M000250769

An Introduction to
Media Literacy
. . . .

by **Lori Moses**
Second Edition

Kendall Hunt
p u b l i s h i n g   c o m p a n y

Cover and interior images © Shutterstock, Inc.

www.kendallhunt.com
Send all inquiries to:
4050 Westmark Drive
Dubuque, IA 52004-1840

Copyright © 2008, 2021 by Lori Moses

ISBN 978-1-7924-2342-0

Published in the United States of America

Table of Contents

Part I

Chapter 2   Media and Culture

Chapter 3   Basic Communication Theory and the Color Wheel Model of Media Communication   37

Part II

Chapter 4   The Component of Construction   51

Contents

Chapter 5   The Component of **Structure**   79

Chapter 6 The Component of **Creative Language**   107

Chapter 7 The Component of Media Operations   141

Contents

Chapter 8 The Component of Message Processing 193

Chapter 9   The Component of **Action**   211

Part III

Preface

● NEW EDITION, NEW CONTENT

This new edition includes a new Media and Culture chapter focusing on comparing media regulation and ownership in the United States as well as in other parts of the world. Because our means to access media is greater than ever before the new chapter also assesses our media consumption as we connect to new media without the traditional constraints.

Therefore we assess our media consumption, including social media, evaluates brand awareness and the affect on cultures worldwide. Additionally, there has been some revisions to the chapter organization, fine tuning of the previous chapter content and updating of resources.

● ALWAYS A WORK IN PROGRESS

This book as well as any study of the media will always be a work in progress as the media continually changes. Media ownership changes constantly through mergers and acquisitions, new forms of media continue to be developed, and ever changing pop culture will always be integrated into mediated messages. The premise of this book is to evaluate these messages and media trends while analyzing the effects on society.

● WHAT THE BOOK IS DESIGNED TO DO

This book is still meant to give students an introduction the major concepts of media and media literacy and to create an awareness for the impact media has on our society while developing an appreciation of the intricacies of media messages. Although it is meant to be an introductory exploration of media literacy, it is still extensive in its scope.

The book will lead students through the creation of media messages paying close attention to the strategic choices that are made, the careful placement within the media, and to the varied responses from an audience. While it will introduce students to a variety of theories, it is designed to be more practical in its approach to media literacy. However this is not a simply a theoretical approach as there are many visual examples used whenever possible to emphasize the various points raised throughout.

◉ ORGANIZATION OF CHAPTERS

Each chapter begins with a set of objectives outlining the educational goals and is accompanied by a concept checklist that together can serve as self-assessment tools.

The summaries at the end of each chapter serve to highlight the major points raised within the chapter and a list of resources will aid in extended research and discovery. Study questions and activity suggestions will also serve to supplement student learning and classroom discussion.

A glossary of terms is provided to expand comprehension of the concepts and theories introduced in the chapters.

Part I contains chapters that offer an introduction to the primary concepts of media literacy, media ownership and regulation, media consumption and use, basic communication theory, and the Color Wheel Model itself.

The chapters in Part II correlate with each of the individual components of the Color Wheel Model. Each component is designed to focus on a major tenet of media literacy while exploring a variety of concepts within each area. A variety of communication theories will be introduced throughout the different areas while examples will be used to demonstrate the characteristics of media messages.

Part III offers source information and resources.

◉ EXTENDED USE OF THE BOOK

While the main focus of the book is on media education, specifically media literacy, there are further implications to rhetorical studies. Much of the evaluation and analysis demonstrated in media literacy explores the same approaches found in rhetorical criticism. Aristotle's canons of rhetoric are introduced as an integral part of the second component of the Color Wheel Model and concepts used to conduct a content, textual, or discourse analysis are equally relevant.

This book is not an attempt to break new ground in media literacy or to expose new research but to outline the major points in media literacy education by gathering the information in a concise manner that will help students build the skills to become media literate. The focus is on the application of the concepts through example and explanation rather than a theoretical approach.

● ACKNOWLEDGMENTS

Many thanks to my colleagues at Monroe Community College in Rochester, NY who not only encouraged me to continue to pursue my passion regarding media literacy but embraced it.

Much appreciation also goes to my students who accepted the challenge of thinking critically about the media they so ferociously consume. I learn as much from them as I hope they do from me.

Most of all to my children Ryan and Erin, who have been an inspiration to me as both a parent and a teacher.

What Is
Media Literacy?

Chapter Objectives

- Define media literacy.
- Summarize the history of media literacy.
- Identify the core concepts and questions of media literacy.
- Describe the importance of acquiring media literacy skills.
- Identify the many texts that can be used in media literacy.

• •

◉ THE PERVASIVENESS OF MEDIA

Though we have lived in a media-driven society for a number of years, the proliferation of the smart phone allows the average American to carry a means to connect to media on their person. As such, the amount of time spent with media has increased each year.

As of this writing, multiple studies have determined that the average American adult now spends a little more than half of the day consuming media–an average of 12 hours and 9 minutes.[1] The data accounts for our media multitasking, counting our use of two different forms of media simultaneously as two hours.

This growth in media consumption is not surprising given the mass ownership of smart phones and 24 hour connectivity. However, with the pervasiveness of media, and the content that we are inundated with, we have no formal means in which to educate ourselves in how to analyze these messages. Media literacy is a means to create more critical media consumers.

◉ DEFINING MEDIA LITERACY

It is common to identify basic literacy skills as the ability to read and write. If we apply those same basic literacy skills to media messages then one who is media literate should have the ability to read and write, or more concisely, to comprehend and create media messages. However, as media literacy has expanded so has this simplistic definition.

In 1992 a more formal definition was developed at the Aspen Media Literacy Leadership Institute Conference, which states that a media literate person has the ability to access, analyze, evaluate, and produce media.[2] Many groups active in media literacy advocacy have since created their own definitions expanding on the four basic tenets of access, analyze, evaluate and produce. These will be explored later in the chapter.

In essence media literacy is an educational approach with the purpose of empowering people with the ability to use critical thinking skills when consuming media thereby creating an awareness for the characteristics of the media, the intent of its messages, the techniques used, and its impact on society. The goal is to develop both an awareness, and appreciation, for the creation of media messages. Supporters of media literacy encourage media education as a means to not only create an informed consumer through the analysis of media content, but also the ability to produce independent media messages.

Media literacy is seen as an investigative process where people are given the skills to recognize artistry, persuasion, bias, and censorship. The idea is that in exploring the meaning behind the messages in print or electronic media one can be more informed and indeed empowered to make better decisions and thereby become better citizens. Media literacy creates an awareness to look beyond the face value of a message, to ask further questions, to identify what isn't being addressed, and to look for answers, or other points of view, from a variety of sources.

The skills developed in media literacy education are part of a lifelong process of evaluation and assessment. Therefore, media literacy is not an inoculating approach to media education where an "immunity" to media messages is produced. In the same vein media literacy is not merely an attack on the media, nor does it call for media censorship. It does advocate for individual choices and perspectives, as well as critical consumption.

Media literacy empowers people with critical thinking skills to consume media with awareness and appreciation.

◉ HISTORY OF MEDIA LITERACY

The media literacy movement was an evolutionary process beginning as far back as the 1930s when the popularity and power of the media raised concerns over its effect on society. Decades of research studies led to the development of various approaches to media aware-ness through the 1950s until the introduction of media education class-es in the 1960s and 1970s.

Media education in the form of media literacy then experienced an international expansion in the 1980s and 1990s. Media literacy is still developing in the United States where it has not received the same amount of formal recognition that has been attained in Great Britain, Australia, Scandinavia, Germany, and Canada, yet ironically the con-cern over the media's impact increases.

Research studies dating back to the early 1930s were commissioned to determine the impact of media on society in general and children in particular. Concerns surrounding the success of the film industry in the late 1920s and its volume of gangster films prompted a major study on the effect of film on children. The Payne Fund Studies, published in 1933, concluded that film did indeed have powerful effects on young audiences and also contributed to criminal activity.[3] The introduction of television gave way to studies in the 1950s, which demonstrated that television had an impact on everything from family togetherness, eating habits, and even the design of the American home.

In 1953, the first national media literacy organization in the United States was formed. Originally named the American Council for Better Broadcasts, the group changed the name to the National Telemedia Coun-cil in conjunction with their thirtieth anniversary in 1983.[4] The organiza-tion continues their work today.

The growth of the media continued to prompt further research re-garding the media's influence on the American public. Among them were studies by the Surgeon General, the American Psychological Association, the American Medical Association, American Academy of Pediatrics, and countless other individuals and organizations. The abundance of media research fostered the organized study of media issues beginning in the 1930s, developing into the formal academic subject of media studies by the 1960s.

In the 1960s, alternative media outlets arose as mainstream media shunned the messages in pop culture declaring them as harmful. The world was experiencing a shifting of philosophies and values. The re-sulting paradigm shift caused an embrace, and the subsequent formal study of, both pop culture and the media. Perhaps no one can be better credited with making media part of pop culture than Marshall McLu-han.

A professor at the University of Toronto, McLuhan foresaw the im-pact of television, its psychological effects, media manipulation, and the use of mediated rhetoric. His ideas were both radical for the time and prophetic. He coined terms such as the "global village" recognizing that the world would become an interconnected community long before personal computers entered our lives. While these catchphrases made him popular with the public, scholars were skeptical of his significance. His most accepted work *Understanding Media: Extensions of Man* was a chronological view of the consequence and characteristics of the development of literacy. Although controversial, McLuhan made media studies part of pop culture becoming part of pop culture himself by "making history–and hysteria–with [his] radical view of the effects of electronic communication upon man and the twentieth century."[5]

This popularization of media studies created a boost in media education around the world in the 1970s. Media education classes were formally introduced into elementary school curriculum's throughout Europe. In 1977, Barry Duncan created the Association for Media Literacy based at the University of Toronto in Ontario, Canada. The organization still sponsors workshops and conferences and creates support materials for media literacy teachers in Canada.[6]

The media literacy movement gained its greatest advances in the 1980s and 1990s when countries like Canada, Sweden, Finland, Denmark, and South Africa mandated media literacy as part of the national school curriculum. Media literacy curriculum varies throughout Great Britain and the Australian states where it is often offered as separate courses.

In 1990 a World Conference in Media Literacy was held in Guelph, Ontario, Canada, where educators from around the world gathered to discuss and implement plans to further media literacy.[7]

While great advances were being made elsewhere, the media literacy movement was moving much slower within the United States. One of the great strides toward media literacy was the creation of the Center for Media Literacy founded by Elizabeth Thoman in Los Angeles in 1989.[8] The Center for Media Literacy continues to offer extensive resources for instructors and scholars of media literacy.

Despite the concerted efforts of several individuals the idea of media literacy needed greater definition and clarity to be taken seriously in education. The National Leadership Conference held at the Aspen Institute in 1992 gave media literacy the boost it needed in the United States. The collaboration of those gathered at the conference resulted in a report that provided a framework for media literacy in education to move forward.[9] Three national media literacy conferences followed as the movement gained momentum and recognition in the United States.

Further support for media literacy resulted when a 1999 report by the

American Academy of Pediatrics on media exposure called for the exploration of mandating media education in American schools.[10]

In 1997 the Partnership for Media Education (PME) was founded and eventually adopted the name the Alliance for a Media Literate America in 2000. The national membership organization changed its name again, in 2008, to The National Association for Media Literacy Education, but its mission remains the same, as an organization dedicated to advancing media literacy.[11]

The controversial Common Core State Standards were introduced in the U.S. in 2009, as an attempt to create consistent K-12 educational expectations across the 50 states. These standards include expectations throughout that could be associated with media literacy concepts, yet not explicitly so. Moreover, while Common Core has been adopted by most states, it has not been adopted by all.[12]

Despite the progress made in the United States, media literacy lags far behind other countries with its sporadic approach to media education.

◉ MEDIA EDUCATION

Literacy skills are a basic aspect of any school curriculum as students are taught to read, write, and comprehend messages in various traditional texts. A Kaiser Family Foundation study found most children spend more time with media than in school, and far more time with media than their parents. The 2010 study, revealed that young people between the ages of eight and eighteen spend an average of 10 hours and 45 minutes a day with all forms of media, equaling over 75 hours a week, the equivalent of two full-time jobs.[13] A study conducted

American media is essentially an unofficial curriculum for children as the US does not regulate media in regard to children as in other countries.

by Common Sense Media in 2015, indicated that tweens and teens spend 5 and 7½ hours per day respectively just on screens.[14] Media is essentially an unofficial curriculum without an instructor.

While the pervasiveness, and often intensity, of media messages are often a cause of concern among media critics, parents, and educators, and health care professionals, there is an irregular approach to media education in the United States. Though media literacy is a required part of the K–12 curriculum in many developed English-speaking countries such as England, Canada, and Australia, it is a foreign concept for most Americans. Media literacy education in American high schools and institutions of higher education are often offered only as electives or may be integrated into the English language arts curriculum.

Unfortunately, the Common Core State Standards do not specifically identify media literacy expectations though several standards can be achieved with the integration of media texts. Though NAMLE has created guides to help educators make the "foundational connections to media literacy education." [15]

While almost all fifty states support media literacy education in some form, it varies drastically by state. The muddled attempts may include issue based concerns such as gender issues, tobacco/alcohol advertising, and media violence, or the attempts may be skills-based involving the production of media such as video production, photography, and desktop publishing. Still another attempt is to use media as an alternative text, teaching with media rather than about media.

Media education must explore the many concepts and characteristics of media. Introducing the subject of media literacy, its intent, and the framework on which the program has been developed is imperative to laying a foundation for media education.

◉ MEDIA LITERACY CONCEPTS

There are several principles media literacy education has been built on—*access, analyze, evaluate, produce* and *act.*

ACCESS

The premise is that in learning to access media one can gain entry to new forms of information and not rely on single or limited sources. Many municipalities have only a single newspaper, a few television stations, and a handful of radio stations in which to acquire news and information. They

KEY CONCEPTS AND QUESTIONS
UNLOCKING MEDIA LITERACY

Each area is accompanied by a central statement and a question that guides the investigative process. Many practitioners have created modifications of the key statements and questions to suit their own models and the Color Wheel Model is no exception.16 The following are the key concepts and questions as they relate to the Color Wheel Model and will be explained more thoroughly in the next chapter.

Key Concepts

1. All media messages are constructed.

2. Media messages have a distinct structure or framework.

3. Media messages use a creative language.

4. Media messages are constructed to gain profit and/or power and have embedded values and points of view.

5. Different people experience the same message differently.

6. Media messages are created to influence an audience response.

Key Questions

1. How was this message constructed and by whom?

2. Who is the target audience and how was the message tailored to them?

3. What techniques are used to attract attention?

4. What lifestyles, values, and points of view are represented in or omitted from this message?

5. How might different people understand this message differently from me?

6. Why was this message sent and how does it impact the audience?

provide for few sources and points of view to equip an audience to be a well-informed citizenry. By learning to access a greater variety of sources, one can piece together information to achieve greater understanding and insight.

With constantly changing technology, our means by which to gain access to the media is increasing. Accessibility to media includes traditional means such as the aforementioned newspapers, television, and radio but many of them have converged with technology to create new means to connect. Online versions of these traditional forms of media allow for expanded connectivity with podcasts, viral video, databases filled with information, and much more. While the Internet provides endless accessibility to information both local as well as global, there is a technology gap that is created when one has limited access or a lack of exposure to newer technologies.

ANALYZE

The analysis of media allows one to examine the structure and contents of a message. A greater awareness and appreciation for media messages can be gained when determining what elements are used to create these packages. Through both prior experience and education, one learns to identify facts, fallacies, and opinions as well as the purpose of the message. Messages can be developed for informational, entertainment, educational, or persuasionary purposes. Understanding that these messages occur within a social, political, and above all, a commercial environment is to understand the implications of these messages and their impact on society.

EVALUATE

The evaluation of a media message occurs when a judgment is made about its content. Despite the ability of the media to reach a mass audience, the evaluative process becomes very individualized as decisions or conclusions are based on one's own values, attitudes, beliefs, and lifestyle choices. Because a message attains greater acceptance when there is greater relevance to the audience, messages are often tailored to that audience.

PRODUCE

The skill to produce or create original, independent messages is a crucial step to becoming media literate. While the ability to "read" messages through analysis and evaluation is imperative, the ability to "write" messages completes the process. The power to deconstruct a message is balanced when one must determine the choices and strategies to use in the creation of a message, resulting in a better insight and appreciation for the process.

ACT

The National Association for Media Literacy Education recently added this concept to their definition, which aligns perfectly to the last component of the model that will be used throughout the book, and was developed by the author almost two decades ago. The premise is that as we consume, interpret, and process media messages, we also react to them. Those actions can be based on our values, attitudes, and beliefs, as well as our level of motivation. The responses can be as varied as those individuals, or groups, that are stimulated by them.

⬤ ACQUIRING MEDIA LITERACY SKILLS

Obtaining any new skill requires opening our minds to something new, to try something we have not attempted before, to be curious, to ask questions. It is the same with acquiring the expertise needed to become media literate, we have to look deeper, to better understand and acknowledge the world around us.

Though we have more information at our fingertips than ever before, if we only choose to consume what is entertaining to us, we will never gain a vast store of acquired knowledge. We must be committed to gathering information from a variety of sources so as not to find ourselves uninformed and biased, based on partial or inaccurate information.

By opening ourselves to alternative messages, we also need to develop critical thinking skills so that as we are exposed to a variety of points of view, we can analyze them, question the issues, determine their implications and consequences, identify fallacies, exaggerations, or omissions, and to make our best determinations for ourselves, in other words, to be critical consumers of information.

⬤ THE TEXTS OF MEDIA LITERACY

Any form of print or electronic media may be explored using the key questions. Typical media texts include images, film, television, newspapers, magazines, websites, comics, podcasts, social media posts, and advertisements. Identifying the signs, symbols, images, and sounds that are used as well as how popular culture is integrated into them is part of the process.

⬤ CONCEPT CHECKLIST

media consumption	media literacy	access
evaluate	analysis	produce
critical thinking	act	media texts

⬤ SUMMARY

- Media literacy is an educational approach with the objective of teaching critical thinking skills to empower people with a greater awareness for the characteristics of the media, the intent of its messages, the techniques used, and the impact on society.

- Although media literacy is a required part of the K–12 curriculum in many developed English-speaking countries, there is no formal approach in the United States.

- Media literacy developed out of concern for the level of influence the media had on society.

- Decades of research studies dating back to the 1930s described the media's effect and led to media awareness programs and eventually to a formal academic subject in the 1960s.

- After an expansion outside of the States in the 1970s, media literacy began to gain momentum in the 1980s and 1990s.

- Several national organizations were formed both in the United States and Canada.

- Five major concepts for media literacy are: access, analyze, evaluate, produce and act.

- There are five exploration areas when analyzing a text: authorship, format, audience, content, and purpose.

- Key concept statements and questions guide the investigative process and a variety of texts may be used.

⬤ ASK YOURSELF ACTIVITIES

1. Ask yourself: How much media do you consume?

Keep a log of your media consumption. First, estimate the number of hours you believe you spend with the media on an average day.

Then document every time you engage with media by logging your media activity for several days. Try to log activities during the course of the week and the weekend. Record each medium you use and the total time (in hours and minutes) that you spent engaged with that medium.

Based on your log information, was your estimate accurate about the amount of the media you regularly consume? On what medium do you spend the most time (radio, television, Internet)? Why? What did you think about the content you consumed? Was it valuable? Accurate? Available elsewhere? Is there anything about your media consumption that you would like to change? What and how?

2. **Ask yourself: What does your digital footprint reveal about you? What kind of media messages are you creating?**

Review your social media accounts. What messages have you posted? How would an outsider perceive you if they only have the information from these accounts?

Google yourself. What did you find out about yourself? Was there any information that surprised you? Was there any information that you did not post yourself?

How public is your private life?

3. Search the Internet for media literacy resources and create a list of those sources with extensive information that might be useful throughout the study of media literacy. Make sure to reference the sources listed in the resources area of the chapter.

⦿ RESOURCES

The following resources are only a few of the excellent online sources for media literacy and much of the information below comes directly from their websites.

The Henry J. Kaiser Family Foundation
www.kff.org

The Kaiser Family Foundations a nonprofit, private operating foundation focusing on the major health care issues facing the United States Many of their research studies have focused on how media has impacted children.

Center for Media Literacy
www.medialit.org

The Center for Media Literacy (CML) has been a pioneering force in the development and practice of media literacy in the United States. It is perhaps the most comprehensive resource for media literacy educators and offers a free download of the MediaLit Kit.

National Association for Media Literacy Education
www.namle.net

The National Association for Media Literacy Education (NAMLE), formerly the Alliance for a Media Literate America (AMLA), is a national membership organization dedicated to advancing the field of media literacy education in the United States.

Common Sense Media
www.commonsensemedia.org

Common Sense Media is a non-profit organization that offers curriculum and toolkits to educators as well as reviews of various media for parents. They also are involved in legislative advocacy and creating public awareness.

The Association for Media Literacy
www.aml.ca

The Association for Media Literacy is made up of teachers, librarians, consultants, cultural workers, and media professionals concerned about the impact of the mass media on contemporary culture. It provides a newsletter, workshops and conferences, and publishes curriculum and support material.

National Telemedia Council, Inc
www.NationalTelemediaCouncil.org

A professional, nonprofit organization promoting media literacy education through partnerships with educators, informed citizens, and media producers across the country.

Media Education Foundation
www.mediaed.org

The Media Education Foundation produces and distributes documentary films and other educational resources to inspire critical reflection on the social, political, and cultural impact of American mass media.

⦿ ENDNOTES

1. Dolliver, Mark. 2019. "Average Time Spent with Media in 2019." emarketer. May 30. Accessed February 19, 2020. emarketer.com.

2. National Leadership Conference on Media Literacy, Aspen Institute, Conference Report, 1993.

3. The Payne Fund Studies, named for the organization that funded the grant, were a series of research projects designed to analyze the influence of motion pictures on children. Begun in 1929 the findings were published in 1933.

4. "Our History." National Telemedia Council . Accessed February 19, 2020. https://www.nationaltelemediacouncil.org/our-history.

5. Quote from the back cover of *Understanding Media: The Extensions of Man* by Marshall McLuhan. (New York: Signet Books, 1964).

6. "Our History." National Telemedia Council . Accessed February 19, 2020. https://www.nationaltelemediacouncil.org/our-history.

7. DeBoer, Ron. n.d. "The Media Literacy Movement: Fledgling to Full Flight." Ontario Media Literacy. Accessed February 19, 2020. http://www.angelfire.com/ms/MediaLiteracy/History.html

8. "About." Center for Media Literacy. Accessed February 19, 2020. http://www.medialit.org/about_cml.html.

9. "Aspen Institute Report of the National Leadership Conference on Media Literacy," Center for Media Literacy, http://www.medialit.org/reading_room/article582.html

10. American Academy of Pediatrics, Committee on Public Education, "Media Education," *Pediatrics* Vol. 104, no. 2 (1999): 341–342

11. "About." Center for Media Literacy. Accessed February 19, 2020. http://www.medialit.org/about_cml.html.

12. "Standards in Your State." Common Core State Standards Initiative. Accessed February 19, 2020. http://www.corestandards.org/standards-in-your-state/.

13. Victoria J. Rideout, M.A. Ulla G. Foehr, Ph.D. and Donald F. Roberts, Ph.D. 2010. "GENERATION M2 Media in the Lives of 8- to 18-Year-Olds." Kaiser Family Foundation. January. Accessed February 19, 2020. https://www.kff.org/other/report/generation-m2-media-in-the-lives-of-8-to-18-year-olds/.

14. Victoria Rideout, M.A. and Michael B. Robb, Ph.D. 2019. "The Common Sense Census: Media Use by Tweens and Teens, 2019." Common Sense Media. Accessed February 19, 2020. https://www.commonsensemedia.org/research/the-common-sense-census-media-use-by-tweens-and-teens-2019.

15. "MLE & Common Core Standards." National Association for Media Literacy Education. Accessed February 19, 2020. https://namle.net/publications/mle-common-core-standards/.

Media and Culture

Chapter Objectives

- Compare U.S. media regulation and ownership to other countries around the world.
- Examine the level of media concentration that exists.
- Discuss how media has influenced our culture and the perception of the US
- Identify how evolving media has impacted cultural change
- Discuss how journalism has changed
- Explain how to counteract fake news and misinformation.

● THE RISE OF MEDIATED CULTURE

Media culture refers to the influence, and impact, the developing media of the 1900s had in not only creating a culture of capitalism in Western society, but how it has had a global impact in changing value systems around the world. While changes in traditional media occurred throughout the last century, we have seen an explosion of new technology which has accelerated the globalization of our media, our brands, and our culture.

Americans often find our culture, our media depictions, and the values within it, so ubiquitous that they believe that the rest of the world has the same values, culture, and nuances as if they were universal.

This chapter is meant to be a brief overview comparing our media culture to that around the world, as well as an abridged look at media regulations, the creation of media conglomerates, and the resulting corporate culture of media, brand imperialism, the impact of emerging media, societies changing behaviors and value systems, including the rise in consumerism. More detailed information regarding the development of American media can be found within chapter 7.

⦿ THE CORPORATE CULTURE OF MEDIA

American Media

Media in the United States is somewhat unique from the rest of the world for three distinct reasons: legal protections, private ownership, and broad regulations.

At the heart of our government is the Constitution, containing the principles and guidelines which create the foundation for the laws of the land. Though this document has been modified, or amended, 27 times, the First Amendment holds particular interest regarding the media. The five freedoms addressed within the First Amendment include the freedom of speech, assembly, religion, press, and the right to petition the government.

No other country began with anything as extensive as the First Amendment, though other countries have since added provisions for freedom of the press and speech within their laws and regulations. However, several countries still censor media content despite the provision. In the United States, by law, the media is protected in providing information, with a few exceptions, but the law also prohibits censorship.

Unlike several other countries, we have no government owned or subsidized media. American media is held privately, by individuals, or more accurately by corporate entities. Canada, the United Kingdom, Australia, Sweden, Germany, France, China and Russia are just a few examples of countries which have state or government owned or subsidized media. While several countries like Canada and England, have a combination of state subsidized and privately held media, there are countries with more extreme cases with few privately owned media. Countries that had state media monopolies like Russia and China are beginning to allow controlled forms of private media while North Korean media remains among the most restrained.

Media regulations differ widely from country to country. In the United States, regulations state that no one owns the airwaves, therefore broadcasters on those airwaves do so in the public interest. The Federal Communications Commission (FCC) is the regulatory body that issues operational licenses, and enforces the broadcast regulations and ownership limitations in the United States.[1]

The passing of the Telecommunications Act of 1996 was a turning point, as it would dramatically change the trajectory of media ownership, allowing media owners to diversify their holdings beyond a single form of media to own additional forms of media.[2] For example, Prior to 1996, a newspaper company could own several newspapers in various markets, but only newspapers. The passage of the Act, allowed that newspaper company to acquire a television or radio station–or both. The deregulation that resulted from the Telecommunications Act of 1996 created the explosive beginning of the media conglomerate and the corporate media culture.

Rupert Murdoch, is an example of a media owner who took advantage of the deregulation, here and elsewhere. Having already assessed a larger number of papers in his native Australia, and nearby New Zealand, he came to the United States to expand his media holdings. He soon discovered that foreign ownership of television stations was frowned upon, so to meet his objectives he would need to change his citizenship, and he did. He began by acquiring metro newspapers including the New York Post, then the 20th Century Fox film studio, before moving to the purchase of a group of over 10 television stations that would initiate the Fox Television network. Additionally he would acquire ViacomCBS, and much more. And so the multimedia conglomerate of Murdoch's company, NewsCorp, started its trajectory to becoming one of the most powerful in the country and one of a handful of media conglomerates that own most of the media in America.

NewsCorp's greatest achievement was the purchase of the Wall Street Journal which had previously only been family owned and operated since it's inception in 1889.[3] More recent changes shifted the focus back to publishing, as Murdoch and his family have sold off significant holdings including the 20th Century film studio, and are outlined in greater detail in Chapter 7.[4] Still, Murdoch's News Corp is among the few companies that control most of the US media.

Canadian Media

Media consolidation is not unique to the United States. While the government subsidized, Canadian Broadcasting Corporation (CBC), is the oldest existing broadcasting network in Canada, they also have several privately owned networks. Despite the combination of state and private media ownership, the country also experienced a large number of mergers and acquisitions, so that they too now have a concentration of their media controlled by only a handful of conglomerates. Just as in the United States, these corporations have diverse media portfolios beyond radio and broadcast television, to include cable television, newspapers, telephone, and more.

The Canadian Radio-television and Telecommunications Commission (CRTC) is the Canadian agency charged with regulating broadcast media (radio and television) and telecommunications (telephone and cell service) but does not have the same jurisdictional range of the FCC, their American regulatory counterpart. In fact, there are several agencies in Canada that regulate different aspects of the media.

Much of the early efforts centered on creating national networks across their vast country so as to serve more Canadians with quality broadcasting. However, the commission has been heavily focused on broadcasting content with a significant emphasis on the promotion and maintenance of the cultural foundation of Canada. In particular, they set their sights on limiting foreign content primarily from the United States. With concern regarding an extensive shared border between the two countries, and several American stations within broadcast range, the CRTC has instituted a number of regulations ensuring the production of Canadian content, limitations on foreign content, and even prohibiting their citizens from adapting equipment to pull in U.S. stations. Simultaneous substitution, is an example of the content protections, the CRTC requires. Simultaneous substitution, or signal substitution, is the practice that requires a Canadian media distributor to broadcast the signal of the local area instead of the foreign broadcast, even when the two stations are broadcasting the same programming simultaneously. For instance, when watching a popular American television show, or even the Super Bowl, in Canada one will see different commercials, and the local station's call sign.[5] Canadians are also prohibited from modifying televisions and radios to receive US broadcasts, however many have found loopholes to this regulation with digital media ,and even purchase satellite dishes from US providers.

The CRTC has been accused of shifting their focused so intently on

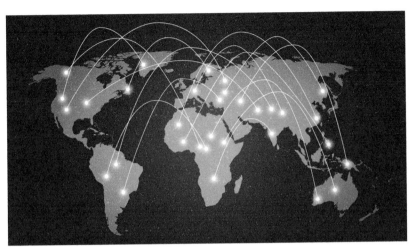

content concerns that it has come under stiff criticism for their failure to control the long list of mergers that occurred over the last decade and a half. As a result, the Canadian Senate commissioned several committees to look into media reform.

Australian Media

Australia is also no stranger to media concentration. In fact, several independent studies have come to the conclusion that Australia has an unusually high concentration of media ownership compared to other liberal democracies and print media ownership, in particular, is much more highly concentrated than that of most other Western countries.[6]

The Australian Communications and Media Authority (ACMA) is the regulatory agency for radio, television, telecommunications and the Internet in Australia, and like the UK, the guidelines for broadcasting and the press are primarily compliance codes that were developed by the industries themselves.

The ACMA also manages the regulations regarding media ownership outlined in the Broadcasting Services Act of 1992. Despite the limits that are in place, the newspaper industry in Australia is dominated by two corporations, one of which is Rupert Murdoch's News Corp.

Australia, is both Rupert Murdoch's native country and where he began his media career, when he inherited the newspapers, and other media entities that his father owned. He would go on create the first national paper, and accumulated several more newspapers throughout the country, and now owns approximately two thirds of the circula-

tion in the dominant metro areas.[7] Additionally, Murdoch is co-owner of the news service, Australian Associated Press (AAP), first established by his father.

An amendment in 2006, relaxed restrictions against foreign ownership and cross-media ownership, and media control by a single company further allowing for more media concentration and the growth of the conglomerates, including Murdoch's.[8]

Australia was but the first step in Rupert Murdoch's global media empire. After Australia, he turned to the United Kingdom to add to his media investments.

Media in the United Kingdom

Like Canada, the United Kingdom, also has private broadcasting networks along with a government subsidized broadcasting network, the British Broadcasting Corporation (BBC). Unlike Canada and the US, the United Kingdom is fairly new to implementing a federal regulatory agency.

Communications Act 2003 places the regulatory responsibilities for broadcasting, telecommunication, and postal services under the control of the newly formed Office of Communications (Ofcom). Prior to 2003, there were two different organizations in the UK that regulated private broadcasters, for primarily licensing, and the codes under which they operated. Both organizations upheld industry developed codes so that in essence, radio and television in the UK, was self-regulated. As a government network, the BBC, is not subject to licensing.

The government can also, request specific information be broadcast, adjust, or even censor, so as to protect national security or the relationships with other foreign governments. It allows any Secretary of State to give secret directions to Ofcom or any providers of public electronic communications networks. They can be instructed "to do, or not to do" any particular thing specified, and the directions do not automatically expire after a certain period. [8]

The Communications Act 2003 provides for the prohibition of political advertising on television or radio, a very foreign concept in America where we are inundated with political ads especially as we inch closer to major local and national elections. Interestingly, another provision, states that Ofcom is responsible to promote media literacy.

Rupert Murdoch set his sights on collecting media in the UK, beginning with tabloid papers, as well as the Times, the Sunday Times, and his largest acquisition–the Sun–the paper with the largest brand reach in the UK. Eventually, he would own a majority of Sky News UK, an extensive news organization that broadcasts via radio and online channels. Here again, Murdoch and his family sold off significant holdings in 2018, including those in the UK. After 30 years, Murdoch parted with Sky TV, selling it to US media corporation, Comcast, thus transferring the major news organization to yet another conglomerate.[11]

Aside from the concern over Rupert Murdoch concentration of media, there was a series of controversies from how he obtained these media outlets without the usual reviews, as well as scandals that surrounded his news organizations like a major phone hacking incident, to influencing elections.

Murdoch is just one of a small group of billionaires that own most of the private media in the UK, and like Canada, many in the UK are concerned by this concentration of media and are calling for reform.

A global media empire

What is most striking, is that Rupert Murdoch was building his media empire on three different continents, simultaneously. Yet, while he concentrated his efforts in the US, the UK, and Australia, Murdoch did not stop there. His media conglomerate, NewsCorp, also invested in a paper in Papua New Guinea, creating the countries first national paper. Another global acquisition was Star India, an Indian media conglomerate, in a country with a population of nearly a billion people. Star India was also sold to Disney under the recent reconfiguration of NewsCorp in 2019.

Further Media Regulation Possible

While all of these countries had some semblance of media regulation, it still did not prevent the onslaught of mergers and acquisitions that created behemoth media corporations from controlling each countries media–and Rupert Murdoch from amassing a global media empire. Many are calling for reforms but it may be too little, too late.

Most of these country's regulatory agencies do not include the press as that is self-regulated through their codes of ethics. Yet there is one form of media that has primarily gone unchecked–social media.

As social media has gone primarily unchecked, many countries around the world are reviewing the possible implementation of regulations, while others have already begun the process.[13] Of primary concern are posts that promote child abuse, illegal activity or terrorism, particularly after such acts were live streamed. Other concerns are cyberbullying, disinformation that can cause harm, hate speech, and fake news.

However, any regulation will need to done carefully so as not to infringe on free speech as some have called for censorship because they find a message disagreeable or even offensive. This can be troublesome as even hate speech–without inciting harm–is protected, as opinions are considered free speech. Determining fake news is another concern, as some claim that bias may determine what is identified as fake news. The hope is that any regulation will still endure our right to free speech and that regulation will be gradual, rather than a broad, far-sweeping approach.

● GLOBAL MEDIA, GLOBAL BRANDS

Corporate media is thriving, as evidenced by Rupert Murdoch's global range and level of media control. With the advent of digital technology, we are no longer limited to the range of a local broadcast. Media is much more global than ever before, except in countries that block or censor information, our media can be accessed and consumed globally. American media, especially film, television, and music is devoured around the world. Foreign consumers of our media have varying perceptions of America and the American lifestyle.

These perceptions are often based solely on our media, unless having actually met Americans or having visited the United States. Several surveys of individuals from primarily Western European countries, revealed that the "Ugly American" is thankfully not a common perception. What was common was that we are loud, polite, but loud. And that we like fast food, and a lot of it–which is why we are fat–but also that we are superficial, vain, rich, and like guns. Those that have visited the US remarked that we like everything big, especially our cars, homes, and food portions. We also love our flag, as it seemed to be everywhere, including our homes,

cars, and clothing. But they also commented about the coveted American lifestyle, the American dream, in the land of opportunity where anyone can become anything, if they put their mind to it.[14]

Brand Imperialism

While our media is consumed globally, so are our brands. Coca-Cola, Pepsi, Levi's, McDonald's, Apple and Disney are just a few of the American brands that have become worldwide powers having achieved such recognition around the world that they have achieved brand imperialism that extends, not just the influence of the brand itself, but also of American culture and lifestyle. Though these brands are popular in other countries, the brands also had to adapt to the foreign culture. In several European countries, Pepsi is sold with a citrus twist, McDonald's serves fries with mayonnaise, and also serves beer. The dominance of these brands exemplifies the idea of brand imperialism. Yet there are others that would say that brand imperialism is not as evident today, as the economy has seen an expansion of global brands.

Of course, many foreign brands have established a consumer base in the US, German car manufacturers Mercedes, BMW, and Volkswagen along with Japanese companies Toyota and Honda, are all a normal part of the American roadways. While shopping for appliances and household electronics it is nothing to see SONY, Bosch, and Samsung alongside General Electric. While living in Germany, the author was amused when shopping at the local market in her small town. There among all of the German foodstuffs were Frosted Flakes and several other American brands, yet just two decades later, while living

in a small town in upstate New York, that same store, ALDI, opened its doors. The world is getting smaller.

Promoting Consumerism

Advertising promotes these brands and the various products. We are persuaded to not only buy the product, but also to buy into the lifestyle. Consumerism is on the rise as we are buying more than what we need, and are going into debt purchasing things we want. McDonald's, Burger King, and Wendy's are in competition with bigger "better" burgers that contain enough calories in one burger than the average person is supposed to consume in an entire day. It is no wonder that obesity is on the rise in America–and why foreigners think we are fat. A further, look into consumerism is explored in Chapter 9.

◉ SOCIAL MEDIA: CHANGING THE WORLD

Social media has had an enormous impact across the world. What seemed like a new form of communication to chat with friends, keep in touch with relatives, and share interests, has become one of the most democratic means of communication, and the primary means to gather and create messages for a vast majority of the public. As previously stated, it is primarily unregulated and open to a variety of uses, both privately as well as commercially.

Traditional media was slow to accept social media as a method to expand their content, and it did not seem like much competition in its earliest stages. Now of course, traditional media has learned to not only accept, but embrace, social media as a way to communicate with the public and extend the traditional media containers. Adding Facebook and Twitter to mainstream media outlets allowed them to communicate directly to their audiences, even before the regular press or broadcast deadlines, and it allowed the average, every day, members of the audience to render their opinions, and enter into discussions.

However, social media is sometimes viewed as competition to traditional media. Media creation and distribution, now lies in the hands of the public and is distributed directly to the same audience. The idea of traditional publishing, newspapers and magazines, are now done digitally through websites, blogs, and even Pinterest. Radio has competition from podcasts, TV has competition from YouTube and various streaming services, while radio competes with playlists that can be built to your specific interests on a variety of services.

Professional Journalism vs. Citizen Journalism

Professional journalism competes with citizen journalism. Citizen journalism, sometimes called street journalism, is an alternative form of reporting performed by amateurs.[16] At its best, citizen journalism can cover stories or create awareness for issues that are not normally covered by the traditional media, allowing for different voices to be heard or emphasizing issues that have gone ignored for too long. This was quite evident as the Hong Kong democracy movement was made more evident in 2019. In a society that is known for controlling information, images of the protests were leaked via social media, alerting the world and traditional media to the ongoing protests. In the United States, the Black Lives Matter movement is one of many social movements that has used social media to create greater awareness, summon sympathizers to participate in protests, and to call for change.

For the average citizen who suddenly finds themselves in the middle of news event, like a natural disaster, or a tragedy, their posts are often the first news accounts of that event, particularly when the situation is simply too widespread for a single reporter to cover. In some cases social media posts may be the only reports shared for hours, or even days, until professional journalists arrive, or the home country is able to broadcast. Visual accounts of the effects of the Japanese earthquake in 2011 and the subsequent tsunami, were primarily sourced from citizens for the first 24-48 hours as video captured from the city was posted on social media. The story continued to unfold as fears of a nuclear meltdown from a damaged nuclear power plant took an already devastating and tragic event to yet another level. Citizens can therefore be-

come contributors to the mainstream media by providing photos, video, and reports thereby broadening coverage.

However, citizen journalism is not without issues. While this kind of dissemination of information is conducted without gatekeepers, the information shared is also done without any guiding principles or controls. Quite often the quality, integrity, and objectivity is called into question. One must be careful as social media messages are often heavily biased, particularly when sensationalizing to provoke more interest, and get more views. One of the reasons so many countries want to regulate social media is due to the amount of misinformation that is shared.

As the COVID-19 pandemic, swept across the world there was no shortage of sound bites and misinformation regarding potential cures, whether to wear a mask or not, how long the virus could live on certain surfaces, whether the younger generation was more immune, if antibodies made one immune, or the absurd suggestions that one should submit infected patients to harmful UV light or flush their systems with bleach. We were learning as we went through the various stages of the virus, and some saw an opportunity to take advantage of the naive and the fearful. With increasing conspiracy theories, and wavering directives, we were dependent on the media to explain the varying reports.

It was the professional journalists in the media who consulted with experts, and committed themselves to their responsibilities to seek the truth by fact checking, and then correcting the rumors and erroneous stories.

The Fourth Estate

Professional journalism is often referred to as the fourth estate, essentially a symbolic fourth arm of the three branches of government – legislative, judicial and executive. Professional journalism performs a very important watchdog function as the fourth estate essentially to promote transparency in the democratic process. Part of that process is also to expose wrong doing by elected officials, whether through illegal or unethical means, the exploitation of power, or sheer incompetence. Journalists also inform the public about issues that they might not be aware of unless they regularly attend town or school board meetings or are tuned into the latest developments in their area.

Professional journalists operate under a code of ethics, are supposed to seek the truth, and acknowledge uncertainties. Journalists should not speculate or sensationalize to incite the audience. While the majority of journalists follow these codes of reporting the truth without bias, an opposing force is also a factor. Competition from various news sources is fierce, and the economics attached to ratings and readership, often eclipses ethics.

This competition, along with the corporate media agenda that develops a bias of its own, has created the dilemma that has been coined as "fake news." The duality of this concept places two concepts against each other—one is the aforementioned inherent bias that a media outlet may take when reporting on certain issues like politics, or misinformation meant to mislead, and the other, occurs when certain parties feel that their perspective is not reported accurately, even when it is.

The Danger of the Sound Bite

Social media and the 24 hour news cycle has changed the way news is reported. We live in the era of the soundbite. A news source may announce tidbits of information as the story unfolds, often with no time to confirm the information being reported, sometimes wavering between fact and assumption. Whereas, the old news cycle allowed for investigation, corroboration of sources, well before you went to press or went on air. Now, stiff competition makes it more important to be first with the information, even if it isn't quite accurate.

For this reason we must be very careful when consuming any kind of information. We must be particularly of the soundbite, and must not base our opinion on an attention getting title or headline without

understanding the context. For this reason again critical thinking is an imperative skill.

⦿ THE CONSUMPTION OF MEDIA

Our consumption of media has changed, not only through the evolution of how the media formats are delivered, but also the sheer volume of information available.

Where once broadcast media was limited to only a few outlets, and even just a few hours in the day. Today we have unlimited access to information, entertainment, and consumer services, through a vast variety of broadcast media, subscription services, cable, satellite, and streaming services, and are able to choose what we consume 24 hours a day. However, with the proliferation of media on demand, our consumption is more self-directed than previous generations. We choose what we want to watch or listen to, as well as when, and how. We can pause it, repeat it, or simply shift to something that interests us more. We live in a media cocoon and while this is self-serving and often self-satisfying, it does not expose us to other ideas, alternative points of view, or to have a greater understanding of the world around us unless we make an effort to do so.

This is unlike the baby boomer generation that was raised with media that they had no control over, like television broadcasts on limited channels, and local radio stations that broadcast the news and music according to their agenda. This generation was exposed to a variety of information whether they liked it or not, but along the way they were acquiring knowledge that could be applied in to a wide variety of concepts and situations.

Originally newspapers, then radio and TV, were the most influential sources of information. In a large metropolitan area, media sources were limited to just three to four television and radio stations, and a newspaper or two. Families gathered around the television or radio to hear events of the day, as well as to be entertained. Newspapers came to the house every day, and were read cover to cover. There wasn't a lot of choice, if you didn't like what was on the handful of television stations, you read a book or listened to records. Though at that time the newspapers, television, and radio stations were all owned by individual companies, we know that today it is the powerful media conglomerates that own multiple media outlets, thus creating the culture of corporate media.

Consumption for Information or Pleasure

Many scholars have seen a vast difference between the acquired knowledge of the Baby Boomer generation to the more focused knowledge of the Gen Xers. The concern is twofold – the lack of exposure to more general knowledge and the reliance on the soundbite. This was enough concern for President Obama to ask the younger generation to examine how they used media–to consume useful information or to be entertained? The concern was that they consumed only what interested them and any information they learned was typically from social media sound bites–without looking any further into that information, and accepting it based on assumption.

One of the best examples of this resulted from the campaigns launched by Bernie Sanders as he tried to gain the Democratic party nomination for President in the 2016 and 2020 elections. The soundbite of a free education was all that was heard as he gained immense popularity with the 18-29 year old demographic, but when questioned no one knew the implications of what a free education would be. After all, it was free. Obviously, nothing is truly free, and someone would have to pay for it. The truth was that to support the plan, $47 billion would be needed, Sanders proposed a tax on Wall Street, specifically investment transactions. Again, for some, it sounded reasonable to tax wealthy Wall Street.[18] But it is not only the wealthy who invest through Wall Street. The average American citizen who has an insurance or pension fund is also an investor, though their dealings are directed through the funds they have named through their employers or investment companies to secure their retirement. To make matters worse the federal funds raised from this proposal would only cover a portion needed, and the individual states would have to make up the rest–approximately a third of the overall cost. How would the states raise these additional funds? Through taxes, of course–and the middle class take yet another financial blow, bearing a greater burden than the rich. [19]

An Informed Citizenry

Here again critical thinking is a key component to moving beyond the sound bite. It is important for an informed citizen to expand their knowledge to read, and consume a variety of information sources to understand more of the world. The liberal arts classes taken in college help to expand that knowledge by creating context and meaning for media messages and an understanding for the world at large.

As we have turned to technology more for entertainment, we have turned away from reading for pleasure and enlightenment. That broader exposure to the written word had further ramifications than the pleasure of a great story. Reading information about different countries and their cultures, or historical references, exposes one to greater awareness, comprehension and diversity.

For those of us who grew up with limited choices in media we watched whatever was on, and it became the foundation of our acquired knowledge. Reading exposed us to new vocabulary, the use of correct grammar, the art of storytelling, and ultimately how to communicate effectively. Our assignments from grade school to college, encouraged access to knowledge, and taught the ability to research for further analysis, to identify relevant information, and to integrate it into our writing.

Today, our exposure is less diverse despite the enormous opportunities because we live in a society driven by popular culture. A culture that is ensconced in the trivial matters of social media whether that's watching cute kittens ride a robotic vacuum or the latest celebrity dance challenge. We have replaced news, art, and culture with reality TV. Most devastating, is the lack of exposure to news around the world.

That is not to say that many people, of all generations, are not still seeking to be informed through legitimate news sources, either through traditional or social media. As those traditional media have embraced the use of social media to extend their reach, we have the ability to be more informed–as long as we read beyond the headline or soundbite.

Though we have more information at our fingertips than ever before, if we only choose to consume what is entertaining to us, we will never gain that vast store of acquired knowledge. We must be committed to an open

mindset, gathering information from a variety of sources so as not to find ourselves uninformed and biased, or with partial or inaccurate information.

By opening ourselves to alternative messages, we also need to develop critical thinking skills so that as we are exposed to a variety of points of view, we can analyze them, question the issues, determine their implications and consequences, identify fallacies, exaggerations, or omissions, to make our best determinations for ourselves, in other words, to be critical consumers of information.

We live in a mediated culture which is why critical thinking is so important. It is why media literacy is imperative to create informed citizens.

⦿ CONCEPT CHECKLIST

media regulation	regulatory agency
media concentration	media conglomerate
mediated culture	global brand
brand imperialism	citizen journalism
fourth estate	watchdog function

social media   soundbite

media consumption   consumerism

fake news   misinformation

open mindset   critical thinking

◉ SUMMARY

- We live in a mediated culture, immersed in a variety of media forms and messages.

- Deregulation, or the loosening of ownership rules, allowed media owners to acquire media entities in various outlets.

- The formation of media conglomerates resulted from the acquisitions and mergers of various media outlets.

- Media concentration has been experienced in several countries, including the U.S., despite media regulations regarding ownership.

- Some major media owners have acquired media outlets in more than one country.

- Media is not contained to the country of origin, and is consumed globally.

- Our media, and advertised brands, create a consumer culture.

- Global brands promote more than the products, they also promote the American lifestyle and culture.

- Social media has changed how we communicate and consume messages.

- Citizen journalism both compliments and competes with professional journalism.

- Professional journalism, also known as the Fourth Estate, performs a watchdog function.

- Thinking critically about media messages makes for an informed citizen.

- Critical thinking can overcome fake news and misinformation.

⚫ ACTIVITIES

1. When reviewing stories, from either professional or citizen journalists, do you access before sharing? is the writer identified, along with their affiliation? are both sides of the issue presented? without exaggeration or bias?

2. Choose a predominant soundbite or headline from a current news story. What assumptions can you make from it? Now research it further by analyzing both sides of the issue. Does that original assumption remain?

3. Do you have an open mindset? Are you willing to attempt new things, including consuming media beyond your favorite go-to outlets? How do you expand your knowledge?

4. Log the media you consume in a day. How much of that media was for entertainment? Was any to gain information and news? Assess the origination of this information–were they professional news sources or the general public?

5. Choose a local broadcast media outlet and research its history. Who is the parent company of that outlet? What else do they own?

6. How do you expand your acquired knowledge base? What books have you read? What Liberal Arts classes do you take?

⚫ RESOURCES

Who owns the Media?
This website by Free Press offers lists of the various media outlets owned by the major conglomerates, <https://www.freepress.net/issues/media-control/media-consolidation/who-owns-media>.

Pew Research Center
The Pew Research Center offers pertinent information about a variety of topics including media ownership, < https://www.pewresearch.org/topics/media-ownership/>.

⊙ ENDNOTES

1. "What We Do." Federal Communications Commission, 10 July 2017, www.fcc.gov/about-fcc/what-we-do.

2. "Telecommunication Act of 1996," Federal Communications Commission, 10 July 2017, https://www.fcc.gov/general/telecommunications-act-1996

3. "Our Businesses: News Corp." News Corp Our Businesses Comments, 2020, newscorp.com/about/our-businesses/.

4. Flood, Brian. "Fox Corporation Becomes Stand-Alone Company as Disney Deal Set to Close." Fox News, FOX News Network, 19 Mar. 2019, www.foxnews.com/entertainment/fox-corporation-becomes-stand-alone-company-as-disney-deal-set-to-close.

5. "Simultaneous Substitution on Cable TV and Satellite." History of Canadian Broadcasting, 2020, www.broadcasting-history.ca/simultaneous-substitution-cable-tv-and-satellite.

6. R Finkelstein, Report Of The Independent Inquiry Into The Media And Media Regulation, 2012.

7. Dwyer, Tim, and Denis Muller. "FactCheck: Is Australia's Level of Media Ownership ..." The Conversation, 11 Dec. 2016, 11.07pm, theconversation.com/factcheck-is-australias-level-of-media-ownership-concentration-one-of-the-highest-in-the-world-68437. *This source links to a report regarding the highly concentrated ownership of Australia's media.*

8. Given, Jock. "Cross-Media Ownership Laws: Refinement Or Rejection?" UNSW Law Journal, Volume 30(1), 2007, pp. 258–268.

9. Huppert, Julian. "1984 Revisited." OpenDemocracy, 13 Aug. 2015, www.opendemocracy.net/en/digitaliberties/1984-revisited/

10. Wallis, Richard; Buckingham, David (10 June 2013). "Arming the citizen-consumer: The invention of 'media literacy' within UK communications policy". European Journal of Communication. 28 (5): 527– 540. doi:10.1177/0267323113483605 (https://doi.org/10.11 77%2F0267323113483605). ISSN 0267- 3231 (https://www.world-cat.org/issn/0267-3231).

11. Waterson, Jim. "Rupert Murdoch's Sky Reign to End as Fox Sells All Shares to Comcast." The Guardian, Guardian News and Media, 26 Sept. 2018, www.theguardian.com/media/2018/sep/26/rupert-murdochs-sky-reign-to-end-as-fox-sells-all-shares-to-comcast.

12. Patel, Shevani. "How Much of the Media Does Rupert Murdoch Own? ." No Majesty, 15 June 2020, nomajesty.com/how-much-of-the-media-does-rupert-murdoch-own/.

13. Sachdeva Sam Sachdeva is Newsroom's political editor, Sam. "How the World Is Tackling Social Media Regulation." Newsroom, 11 Apr. 2019, www.newsroom.co.nz/2019/04/11/531599/how-the-world-is-tackling-social-media-regulation.

14. *The perceptions of Americans was compiled from a variety of sources including the following:*
    a. "How Americans Are Perceived by the Rest of the World." CBS News, CBS Interactive, 14 Aug. 2016, www.cbsnews.com/news/how-americans-look-to-the-rest-of-the-world/.
    b. "20 Weird Things Foreigners Say about Americans from Cultural Quirks to Courtesy and More." USA Today, Gannett Satellite Information Network, 26 Dec. 2018, www.usatoday.com/picture-gallery/travel/2018/12/20/20-weird-things-foreigners-say-americans/2373768002/

15. "Fact Sheets and Brochures." Centers for Disease Control and Prevention, Centers for Disease Control and Prevention, 7 Feb. 2020, www.cdc.gov/obesity/resources/factsheets.html.

16. Radsch, Courtney C. The Revolutions will be Blogged: Cyberac-

tivism and the 4th Estate in Egypt. Doctoral Dissertation, American University, 2013.

17. Min, Seong-Jae (2016). "Conversation through journalism: Searching for organizing principles of public and citizen journalism". Journalism. 17 (5): 567–582. doi:10.1177/1464884915571298 – via SAGE.

18. Archibald, Robert B., and David H. Feldman. "Opinion | Why Bernie Sanders's Free College Plan Doesn't Make Sense." The Washington Post, WP Company, 22 Apr. 2016, www.washingtonpost.com/news/grade-point/wp/2016/04/22/why-bernie-sanderss-free-college-plan-doesnt-make-sense/.

19. Wellman, Mitchell. "Here's How Much Bernie Sanders' Free College for All Plan Would Cost." USA Today, Gannett Satellite Information Network, 17 Apr. 2017, www.usatoday.com/story/college/2017/04/17/heres-how-much-bernie-sanders-free-college-for-all-plan-would-cost/37430393/.

Chapter 3

Basic Communication Theory and the
Color Wheel Model of Media Communication

Chapter Objectives

- Identify the concepts of basic communication theory.
- Compare the linear model of communication to the transactional model.
- Identify the components of the Color Wheel Model of Media Communication.
- Identify and explain the components of the outer wheel.
- Identify and explain the six major components of the Color Wheel Model of Media Communication.
- Examine the inner section of the Color Wheel Model.
- Identify the complementary pairs of the Color Wheel Model.
- Discuss the culminating statement.

◉ WHAT IS A THEORY?

A theory is a series of propositions intended to describe or explain an experience or occurrence and is developed through assumption, research, and observation. Because the premise of a theory may describe what is supposed to happen, or may be possible in a given situation, it can often predict behavior or consequences—in essence, an "if, then" scenario. If consistent, this anticipation of behavior can lead to the control of an event that can then trigger a desired response. Therefore, theories can describe, explain, predict, or control behavior.[1]

Theories also structure for further development and research as well as to create greater awareness of various phenomenon in everyday experiences. Students are often asked to identify a theory in which to guide their research and the investigative study of a topic.

Theories are not reserved for scientists and scholars as we all use theories in our daily lives. We live by various theories that we have developed through our own experiences and observations. For instance we can theorize that the dark and brooding clouds that exist in the sky are a sign of impending bad weather. This premise is based on our past experiences of such an occurrence and may be bolstered by information gathered from other sources such as a weather forecast describing an incoming front. One could further suggest that individuals who have knowledge of the approaching weather would dress for the conditions or suffer the consequences.

⦿ BASIC COMMUNICATION THEORY

Communication theories have been developed, refined, and abandoned for thousands of years. As our access to media has flourished with new technologies, communication theories have been tested for their endurance in an ever-changing media environment. Theoretical constructs, or models, illustrate the basic proposition or hypothesis and describe, explain, and often as previously stated, predict actions or behaviors.

In order to better understand communication in general, an examination of several models is necessary as they are the foundation for the study of media literacy. One of the most common communication models is the *transactional model.*

Communication can be simply described as the distribution of information and that information can be either verbal or nonverbal. But communication isn't that simple as there are obstacles that can hinder the success of communication. By building the model representing transactional communication, the complexities of communication can be examined.

THE TRANSACTIONAL MODEL

To begin there is a sender and a receiver as in *figure 1.* The sender must *encode* or package a message in such a way that he or she believes the message will be interpreted correctly. Much of the time this doesn't take much thought as we converse with others, but there are times when this

Figure 1

can be a bit more challenging like when giving directions to someone unfamiliar with the area. Then we may have to pick our words more carefully and factor in the correct sequence.

The message is sent via a channel that may include everything from one's voice, to a cell phone, or a form of mass media like television. If the channel malfunctions in some way, communication may be compromised.

Once the receiver is presented with the message, he or she must then *decode* or interpret it. If the receiver translates the message, as it was intended by the sender, communication is successful; if not, miscommunication results. Determining whether that interpretation was successful is the next part of the process.

Figure 2

The transactional model is named for the next step. In *figure 2* the process gains a valuable feature with the *feedback loop*. The feedback loop gives the receiver the ability to respond to or interact with the sender; in essence, there is a transaction of information between them. This part of the process allows for a greater possibility of successful communication whether they ask for clarification or comment in some other way.

However, despite the ability to exchange information obstacles still exist to successful communication. One such obstacle is noise as depicted in figure 3. Noise can manifest itself in different forms all of which can hinder communication. [2]

Figure 3

Environmental noise is sounds that can distract from communication like the roaring of a jet overhead or laughter at the next table in the library.

Mental noise is the internal distractions the receiver must overcome to pay attention like daydreaming in class or desperately trying to focus on what someone is telling you although they have something grotesque stuck in their teeth.

The final form of noise is *semantic noise* as depicted in *figure 4*. This is the linguistic interference

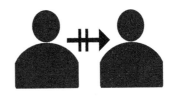

Figure 4

or language differences that can occur when someone uses words or terminology that we do not recognize or is speaking with a very thick accent. A message can also be unclear when the sender uses vague language, perhaps because they are trying to hide something. As a result of semantic noise, meaning can shift and create an undesirable outcome.

As individuals, we each bring our own perceptions to the communication process. The environment in which we were raised and live, our cultural backgrounds, values, attitudes, and beliefs all shape us into who we are and is a decisive factor in the manner in which we encode and decode information. Individual *communication spheres* encompass both the sender and receiver in *figure 5*.

Successful communication can only occur if a common ground can be obtained. The merging of the two communication spheres in the center is this common ground where meaning is obtained through conventional or expected meanings. However, care needs to be taken not to overgeneralize when encoding or decoding messages as this can result in stereotyping.

Identifying the elements of the transactional model is a foundation on which to build an understanding of how mass communication occurs as some of these same elements are present in the model used to depict mass communication.

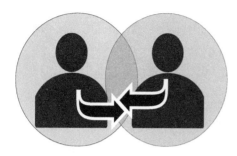

Figure 5

THE LINEAR MODEL

The linear model in *figure 6* contains a receiver experiencing a message from a mass medium. Still present are the message and its channel, the receiver's communication sphere, and noise. Gone is the feedback loop leaving the receiver to decode the information in the message without the benefit of clarification. The receiver can only hope to interpret the message as it was intended or may be left confused if they cannot determine what the meaning was.

Figure 6

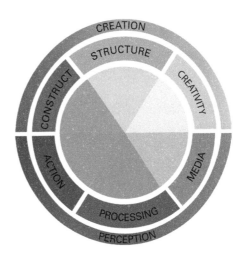

The Color Wheel Model was developed out of necessity as most communication theories were to narrow in their approach.

◉ THE COLOR WHEEL MODEL

Models often use metaphors to illustrate a theoretical hypothesis and the Color Wheel Model of Media Communication does the same. The color wheel many are most familiar with is the circle we were introduced to in art class, with different colored sectors used to show the relationship between colors. The Color Wheel Model of Media Communication also contains different sectors representing the different elements, core concepts of media literacy that were discussed in Chapter 1. As with the original color wheel, the systematic arrangement of the Color Wheel Model of Media Communication will demonstrate the relationship among the different elements. [3]

The Color Wheel Model of Media Communication is the basis for this book's interpretation of the concepts of media literacy. The explanation of the Color Wheel Model in this chapter should clarify the foundational concepts and serve as a preview to the upcoming chapters.

The framework on which this study is based follows the process of media messages beginning with their creation through the interpretive process. This approach is different from most but emphasizes the constructiveness of messages and the deliberateness in their creation. Once a message is created, it must be placed strategically in the media where the media's agenda and value system become an integral part of the process. Here the message is introduced to the audience who process the message in an attempt to interpret the intended meaning and are influenced to respond in a variety of actions. The process is cyclical, because based on the response of the audience the creative process is refined and begins again.

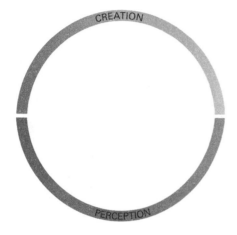

THE OUTER RING OF THE COLOR WHEEL

In simplest terms media messages are a two part process. The creator creates and the consumer perceives. The creator encodes and sends a message, the consumer decodes it. Yet this process is cyclical. There is an element of give and take, of feedback and response. The outer rings of the model indicate this basic aspect of communication.

A distinction needs to be made regarding perception rather than interpretation that will be clarified throughout this approach. Simply stated, accurate interpretations of a designer's creative process may not always occur due to the subjective nature of the perceptual process.

Delving into the wheel's hierarchy is equal parts, each representing elements pertinent to media messages: construction, structure, creative language, media, message processing, and action.

COMPONENTS OF THE COLOR WHEEL

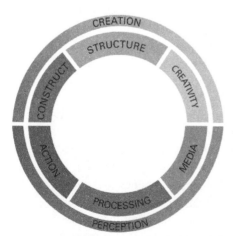

To explain the inner workings of the model, each component will be identified along with the corresponding key media literacy concept and question followed by a brief description of what will be explored.[4] As stated above, the top portion of the wheel deals with the creation of media messages beginning with the Component of Construction.

Construction

Key Concept—All media messages are constructed.

Key Question—How was this message constructed and by whom?

The first principle to grasp is that all media messages are created. It is not a random occurance;

therefore, identifying who created the message and what deliberate choices were made in its creation are a key factor. By deconstructing a message, one can determine what signs and symbols are used, in what context, and their connotative meaning.

Structure

Key Concept—Media messages have a distinct structure or framework.

Key Question—Who is the target audience and how was the message tailored to them?

Message creation is a paradox. What may appear as elusive and arbitrary is actually a very deliberate act with a distinct methodology. Aristotle understood the importance of identifying a target audience and tailoring a message to them. Using the Five Canons of Rhetoric the framework or structure of a message can be identified.

Creative Language

Key Concept—Media messages use a creative language.

Key Question—What techniques are used to attract attention?

In order to compete for our attention, the creators of media messages must use a variety of creative approaches and appeal strategies to grab the attention of the audience and entice them.

Media Operations

Key Concept—Media messages are constructed to gain profit and/or power and have embedded values and points of view.

Key Question—What lifestyles, values, and points of view are represented in or omitted from this message

The second half of the wheel consists of the perceptive elements of the consumer beginning with the element of media.

Media is the channel in which a message is distributed and the consumer, receives that message. That message must be strategically placed within the media to reach the profiled target group. In creating that strategic message, certain lifestyles, values, and points of view are portrayed often through the use of generalizations. In doing so the values and points of view of others are omitted or marginalized and stereotypes may be generated.

Media messages take place in a commercial environment that also has social and political implications. Identifying the agenda of the media and recognizing the scope of the media as a business that exerts power and influence over a mass audience will also be investigated.

A variety of media forms such as film, television, magazines, newspapers, websites, cartoons, and various types of advertising will be examined to identify their unique characteristics and determine how they tell their stories, and to whom.

Message Processing

Key Concept—Different people experience the same message differently.

Key Question—How might different people understand this message differently from me?

Once the consumer receives the message it must be processed. Perception occurs by a process of discerning information, evaluating that information, and determining whether the message aligns with one's individual ideology and lifestyle. Because perception is an individualized process, different people will interpret messages differently.

The psychological processes of perception will be investigated to determine how we accumulate and apply knowledge, how we reason through ambiguity, and interpret messages by identifying patterns. Personality type and individual preferences also factor into the interpretive process.

This component will also cover persuasion, how it occurs, and how the critical thinking skills fundamental to media literacy are a defense against persuasion.

Action

Key Concept—Media messages are created to influence an audience response.

Key Question—Why was this message sent and how does it impact the audience?

The last component on the wheel, action, is the culminating effect of message processing, which requires a judgment based on one's attitudes, values, and ideologies. The subsequent determination results in a response, based on the level of motivation of the audience.

Every message has a purpose and that purpose is to elicit a response or action from the audience. Research has identified different individual responses such as consumer, psychological, and behavioral responses, but there are also mass audience responses, which can then be integrated in social contexts.

The cycle is then complete and based on consumer response messages may be adjusted or created fresh, or the consumer themselves may utilize the cycle to create and communicate independent messages.

◉ THE INNER RING OF THE COLOR WHEEL

What we have accumulated along the way are a set of overlapping attributes from the various components. These are the qualities that were repeated in several components along the Wheel such as target audience, accumulated social knowledge, connotative meaning, signs and symbols, style and cognitive processing. The synthesis of these overlapping factors will create the final level of the hierarchy and the central circle for the theory of visual communication.

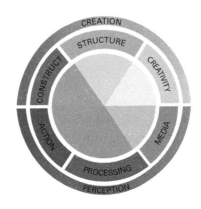

THE CORRELATION TO COLOR THEORY

While the model looks similar to the color wheel from art class, it also behaves like one. In color theory colors opposite each other on the Wheel are complementary in that they work to balance each other. So too does the Color Wheel Model of Media Communication as the pairings illustrate how we are impacted by media messages.

In the interest of simplicity we can demonstrate the complementary pairings of the Color Wheel Model with a concise statement that will summarize the impact of the media and the need for media literacy. By building the statement one pairing at a time the insight of the model will be revealed.

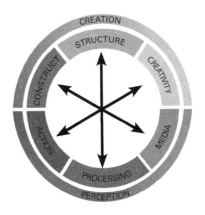

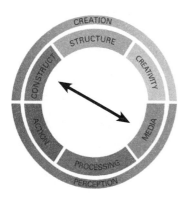

PAIRING CONSTRUCTION AND MEDIA

The statement—*A carefully constructed message, placed strategically in the media, will gain exposure...*

Media messages are carefully constructed creations steeped in symbolism. These messages take many forms and are strategically placed within various types of media. Because media is so pervasive, we are exposed to hundreds of messages a day yet show interest in few. The sheer volume desensitizes audiences to many of these messages unless something about the message makes them take notice.

PAIRING STRUCTURE AND MESSAGE PROCESSING

The statement—*...specific to its target audience so as to motivate the interpretive interest of that audience...*

Message creators know that it takes more to cut through the clutter of media messages. Even Aristotle knew the importance of aligning a message to the target audience. By considering the interests, values, and beliefs of the audience, a message is more likely to hear or see something that intrigues them. Tailoring the message to the audience's interpretive abilities and motivations is significant to elevating that message over the underlying din of all the others.

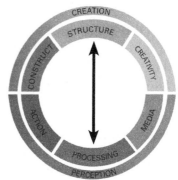

PAIRING CREATIVE LANGUAGE AND ACTION

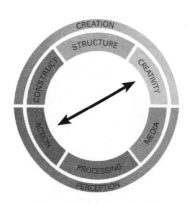

The statement—*...and by using an unusual or unexpected approach is most likely to elicit a greater response.*

Prior to this stage the audience was intrigued because the message was adapted for them but now the message gets a charge of creativity. The more unexpected or creative the approach, the more the audience will notice. Where the attempt in the last pairing deserved a second look, this one commands it. A creative approach that uses innovative or unexpected imagery will attract greater attention, be more memorable, and elicit a greater response.

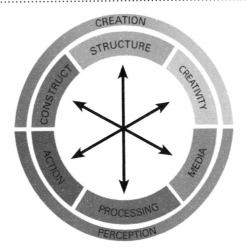

THE COMPLETED THEORETICAL STATEMENT

A carefully constructed message placed strategically in the media will gain exposure specific to its target audience so as to motivate the interpretive interest of that audience and by using an unusual or unexpected approach is most likely to elicit a greater response.

SIMPLE BUT THERE IS MORE BEHIND IT

The above statement is simplistic, but examining media messages through the Color Wheel Model will prove that the concepts are more extensive. This statement is meant to represent all that it takes to craft and interpret a message.

We can summarize that when constructing a message, careful thought goes into the signs that will be used along with their connotative meanings, using a visual hierarchy to attract the audience, and structuring the message along the framework of the canons, while employing a creative twist to entice and appeal to the audience. The media placement must be strategic but we still must be aware that the media agenda is to profit and that motivates certain choices. Audiences are motivated to gather and use information to help them come to decisions using a variety of psychological influences including personality type. Once the audience comes to a decision, they are set to act with any variety of responses.

The cycle is complete and begins again.

⬤ **CONCEPT CHECKLIST**

transactional model	linear model
sender	receiver
message	channel
noise	feedback loop
communication sphere	creation
perception	construction
structure	creative language
media operations	message processing
action	communication theory

Color Wheel Model of Media Communication

⬤ **SUMMARY**

- The transactional model of communication is a representation of the various characteristics of communication.

- Senders encode information and send it via a channel to a receiver who must decode the information.

- A feedback loop allows both the sender and receiver to reiterate and clarify the message.

- Noise in the form of environmental noise, mental noise, or semantic noise can be barriers to successful communication.

- Interpretation is subjective as receivers bring the contents of their communication sphere—their values, attitudes, and beliefs—to the way they perceive a message.

- The linear model depicts the aspects of mass communication; however, one important aspect is missing, the feedback loop.

- The Color Wheel Model of Media Communication is the framework on which this exploration of media literacy is based.

- The outer circle of the Color Wheel Model contains two basic components, creation and perception. They represent the two fundamental aspects of media: (1) that all messages are created or packaged using various strategies, (2) that the audience must try to interpret the message as it was intended but the audience is only as accurate as their own perceptions allow.

- The next level of the wheel consists of six components—construction, structure, creative language, media, operations, message processing, and action.

- The first three components represent the creation aspects of a message. Construction identifies the elements used in a message, Structure determines the framework, and Creative Language the appeal strategies used to gain attention.

- The last three components are about audience perception. Media Operations reveals the media agenda and strategic placement of the message, Message Processing the techniques an audience uses to interpret messages, and Action the responses to messages.

- Each component focuses on a key concept of media literacy, which correlates to a guiding question in the exploration of media literacy.

- The inner wheel of the model consists of the overlapping attributes among the six components.

- The model acts similar to the Color Wheel in art theory as the pairings in this model compliment each other to create the theory.

- The theory states that a carefully constructed message placed strategically in the media will gain exposure specific to its target audience so as to motivate the interpretive interest of that audience and by using an unusual or unexpected approach is most likely to elicit a greater response.

● ASK YOURSELF ACTIVITIES

1. Ask yourself: Are you a good communicator? With a partner, conduct an instructive drawing experiment. One person should obtain a simple illustration from a coloring book or clip art image. This person becomes the instructor who must talk their partner through the drawing of the object without revealing what it is in whole or in part. Instruction should continue through completion of the object. The instructor must give precise directions, and may not look at their partners drawing during the process to offer guidance or clarity. The drawing partner may share their creation only when complete. How close did the finished product resemble the original?

2. At some point in time you have all probably played a version of the "Telephone Game" where a message is whispered in the ear of one participant and they in turn whisper it to the next person. The message is passed from person to person with the last person revealing what they heard. Rarely does the message accurately resemble the original. Why does this miscommunication occur? Try it and see what happens.

3. Watch people engaged in conversation from a distance. Assess their nonverbal communication, body language and facial expressions. What kind of discussion are they having? What emotions are they exhibiting?

4. Repeat the following phrase, "What a wonderful day." Use different tones and inflections to express joy, sarcasm, or boredom. Notice how the meaning can change despite the fact that the words are the same.

5. The book, *Not Quite What I Was Planning; Six-Word Memoirs by Writers Famous and Obscure* by Larry Smith and Rachel Fershleiser asked people to sum up their lives in a six word phrase. Try it.

◉ RESOURCES

Center for Media Literacy
www.medialit.org

The Center for Media Literacy (CML) has been a pioneering force in the development and practice of media literacy in the United States. It is perhaps the most comprehensive resource for media literacy educators and offers a free download of the MediaLit Kit.

National Association for Media Literacy Education
www.namle.net

The National Association for Media Literacy Education (NAMLE), formerly the Alliance for a Media Literate America (AMLA), is a national membership organization dedicated to advancing the field of media literacy education in the United States.

◉ ENDNOTES

1. Dominic A. Infante, Andrew S. Rancer and Deanna F. Womack, *Building Communication Theory* (Prospect Heights, IL.: Waveland Press, Inc., 1997), 39.

2. Ibid., 6.

3. The Color Wheel Model of Media Communication was developed by the author through several unpublished papers.

4. The key concepts and questions of media literary in this book were adapted by the author to correlate the Color Wheel Model and are widely used by are variety of media literacy organizations.

Part II

Chapter 4

The Component of
Construction

Chapter Objectives

- Identify the creator of the message.
- Identify the signs and symbols used as the basic elements in a message.
- Analyze the denotative and connotative meanings of signs.
- Discuss the generalizations that often occur in messages.
- Discuss the need for corporate images to maintain a positive image.
- Analyze the elements used to build trademarks and pictographs.
- Compare the effectiveness of different symbols.

Key Media Literacy Concept #1:
All media messages are constructed.

Key Media Literacy Question #1:
How is this message constructed and by whom?

◉ **MESSAGES ARE CONSTRUCTED**

We give little thought to the media messages we consume on a daily basis. Some may view media as merely a form of entertainment or a source of information, but media messages are much more than that. Media literacy teaches us to take the time to see these messages as texts, and in learning to "read" them we empower ourselves with a greater understanding and deeper appreciation of the media's role and impact on our culture.

To understand that media messages are creations of people who work behind the scenes and make deliberate choices is to begin to perceive the constructed nature of media messages. Message creation is a very complex process that will require the top half of the Color Wheel Model, and several chapters of this book, to explore. Despite its complexity, a well-crafted message often appears effortless and is usually more successful in its ability to communicate. By learning how messages are constructed, we can develop both an appreciation for the effort as well as an awareness for the underlying meaning.

● WHO CREATED THE MESSAGE?

Every media message has a purpose. They are strategically created to affect a response, and by determining who created the message, we are more likely to discover the purpose of the message. All media texts are strategically packaged and are not just elusive or arbitrary creations, but deliberate acts with a distinct methodology. They are designed by creative teams who make distinct choices, determining what images, text, and sounds to include, as well as what to omit through editing, cropping, or rejection.

Most media messages are created in a commercial environment and are carefully planned to serve a purpose.

The local television news crew, the newspaper reporter, the graphic designer, and the writer of your favorite television show are just a few of the people responsible for creating media messages. Many of them work in a team environment where it takes a coordinated effort by a number of people to put a message together.

It is easy to recognize this collaborative effort as the credits roll after the nightly news or a feature film, and it is just as simple to identify the writer of an article in a newspaper or magazine from the byline and the editorial staff listed in the masthead. But the creator of the television commercial or the advertisement in a magazine is less obvious as they are not identified.

The production of a message and the strategic choices made are controlled throughout the process by a hierarchy of individuals, as the writer or designer must answer to the creative director who ultimately responds to the client's desires.

Most media outlets have gatekeepers, such as editors and producers, who control the manner in which the message is packaged and also how it is disseminated to the audience. For example, the local news producer must decide what news stories will air in the limited time available and where in the newscast those stories will be placed. If a breaking story occurs, then a decision about what to bump from the broadcast must be made. This raises the point of omission, in other words, what is not covered or offered in a message, which will be addressed separately in this chapter.

While a team of professionals are required to produce a news cast, television show, or magazine ad, the creators of such messages do so for businesses, corporations, organizations, and institutions, and to identify them is to understand the source of the message. All of these entities have an agenda, and whether it is to boost ratings, perceptions, or sales, the underlying purpose is to profit.

Messages may be packaged as entertainment, information, education, advertising, and persuasion. No matter what form the message takes, or the outlet in which it is placed, it is carefully planned to serve a particular purpose. Determining what kind of images, music or sound to use, or how color and type should be integrated are some of the strategic choices integral to message construction. Identifying the choices made are then necessary to the analysis of a message and can be done by deconstructing the message.

⬤ DECONSTRUCTION

Anything that is constructed can be deconstructed. This act of evaluation and analysis will help to understand the elements used in packaging messages as well as the complexity of the message and its meaning.

To do so we must determine what basic elements are used in a message and how. We can begin an analysis of the visual information. Visual media have the greatest impact because vision is our primary sense, and the basis for our perception and comprehension. An image is more than what is seen on the surface, and is actually a collection of signs and symbols. These signs and symbols are the elemental building blocks of any message and have both denotative and connotative meanings. The first step in deconstructing a message is to identify the signs used and discover their meanings through semiotics.

● SEMIOTICS

The study of signs and symbols is called *semiotics*. Signs are the basis for communication and constitute our written and spoken language as well as the visual images we interpret. A sign designates something to which meaning is attached. For example, a generic picture of a bird can be seen as just that—a bird. A symbol is an object used to represent something abstract, like a concept. A picture of a dove, while also a bird, can be interpreted as a symbol for peace.

Often these visual symbols are viewed as visual metaphors, where an image is compared to a seemingly unrelated subject, like the dove representing peace. However, the meaning of these symbols must be learned, therefore, the key to semiotics is acquired knowledge. In time we learn what labels to attach to objects as well as the appropriate response.

This is called consensual agreement; we have consented or agreed to this representation. The more common the representation, the more successful communication will occur. The dove is a commonly used symbol for peace and is learned at a fairly young age and applied easily. Another example is the traffic light. Most of us were probably toddlers when we learned that when driving a car one should stop if the traffic light is red, and go if it is green. We have consented to abide by this practice, which of course is supported by the knowledge that if we don't, the result could be a traffic ticket.

It is the learned meaning of signs and symbols that led many great semioticians to believe that imagery possessed a language and more

Denotation vs. Connotation— the basic bird pictured here has little meaning, but the second image suggests a symbol for the concept of "peace."

extensively a grammar. Whether the decoding of images entails a complete language may be debatable, yet there are many distinct similarities that make the concept of a visual language possible. Ferdinand de Saussere, Charles Pierce, and Roland Barthes were among the renowned scholars who attempted to find the correlations between the linguistic system and visual communication.

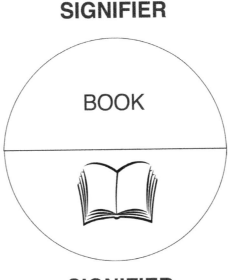

The concept of signifier and signified suggest that a mental image is triggered when seeing, or hearing, any word or "text."

Saussere's work correlated visuals to language, realizing that just as language has denotative and connotative meanings, imagery does as well. Saussere categorized the representations of images as "signifiers" representing the physical entity and "signifieds" representing the conveyance of a concept or emotion.[1]

Roland Barthes was influenced by, and extended, Saussere's concepts, and are perhaps the easiest to apply for our use in explaining the meaning of visual imagery within media messages. Barthes analyzed advertising imagery and their messages in his essay *"Rhetoric of the Image"* noting that the elements used in these images are chosen for symbolic value and their intentional purpose.[2]

As Saussere before him, Barthes also classified images as having two parts—the signifier as the word (in spoken or written form), and the signified as the mental concept or image triggered in the brain. Combined, these two entities create the sign.

Using the example "book," the word is the signifier triggering the mental image or signified. In simplistic terms, whenever we read or utter a word, a correlating image is created in our heads. These fleeting mental images are triggered automatically by our brains and aid in the communicative process, they are how meaning is developed. However, these mental images have a purpose beyond merely identifying objects.

⦿ DENOTATION AND CONNOTATION

The mental image aids in creating meaning; yet meanings applied to symbols may have both a literal or specific meaning (denotation) or an abstract or suggested meaning (connotation). As stated previously, the image of the dove became more than a bird (denotation) but also a symbol of peace (connotation).[3]

In our previous example, the mental image of the book creates a literal or iconic pictorial image in our minds; thus, the denotative interpretation would be similar to what one might find in a dictionary or encyclopedia entry. However, one usually moves beyond this image to other additional suggested or connotative meanings based on the individual's experiences. In this case one might think about a particular book that is a personal favorite, or the last book that they read, or even one's high textbook bill at the bookstore. The connotative meaning is any idea, perception, or emotion that is implied by an individual, in addition to its literal or specific meaning.

This mental impression can be quite powerful and is purely subjective. Barthes noted that the "purely denoted image ... is not possible" [4] that there is always a connotative meaning implied by the reader which completes the relationship between signifier and signified or the denotative element and connotative meaning.

To further illustrate the point that signs have both denotative and connotative meanings, we'll use the word "dog." The mind may evoke an image of a four-legged animal with a tail and ears as pictured. This

When the idea of "dog" is triggered through a text, we understand the basic idea of the four-legged animal (signifier) but may have thoughts of a more personal nature (signified).

mental image creates denotative meaning for the interpreter. But that meaning may expand when connotative elements of a personal nature are added to the image. Perhaps the image of a specific breed is applied when one thinks about a dog that they currently or previously owned. The image may not be quite so pleasant if the memory of a neighbor's incessantly barking dog comes to mind, or there is a fear of the animal triggered by a previous event. Either way these connotative meanings are both powerful, and dependent, on the individual's perception.

Barthes's studies further stated that there is no established system for interpretation of signs as it is left to the interpretation of the individual as determined by their previous knowledge, experiences, and perceptions. Messages must therefore be constructed using signs with some generalized and accepted meaning to be successful. Meaning is both subjective and influenced by an individual's values, attitudes, beliefs, and one's environmental and cultural upbringing. In other words, we bring that communications sphere discussed in the previous chapter with us to decode symbols.

Some symbols are culturally significant to certain countries or ethnic groups while others outside of that group would not have the same response. For example, the American flag may be a symbol of pride for many within the United States, but may be viewed with contempt in other parts of the world. Some symbols like the traffic light are universal, as all over the world where traffic lights are used, motorists stop on red and go on green—even if they drive on the other side of the road!

The traffic light is a universal symbol as it is known the world over. Through consensual agreement we go on green and stop on red.

ANALYZING SIGNS

Any image either illustrative or photographic is a collection of signs and symbols. These signs and symbols are the elemental building blocks of any message. To begin analyzing a message, we must identify the basic denotative elements used without applying any connotative meaning. While this sounds simple enough, it can actually be

Any image is a collection of signs and symbols.

UNIFICATION OF THE KOREAN PENINSULA

Reprinted by permission of Dan Reisinger

very difficult as our interpretive process is second nature. Therefore, when determining the denotative elements, a critical analysis must focus on the text rather than the message. In other words, identify only what you see and not what it means.

Using the example above one sees a torn piece of paper with the word "Korea" printed on it and the tear has been mended by staples. These are the denotative elements or the basic building blocks of the message.

The next step is to determine the connotative meaning behind these signs using knowledge that we have accumulated through both formal study and our personal experiences. In this case, the tear in the paper rips the word "Korea" in two, similar to the division of the country in eastern Asia that is now divided into the countries of North Korea and South Korea. Many efforts at reunification have been attempted over the years with little progress. The attempt to reunify this piece of paper has also been approached in a haphazard manner. The letterforms are ill-aligned and one would hardly attempt the repair of a tear of this magnitude using staples as they would not hold as permanently as tape.

Therefore, one could conclude that the underlying meaning of this message is that the attempts to reunify the countries of North Korea and South Korea have been minimal in their efforts, which will not result in a permanent merger of the two countries. The resulting connotative meaning carries a rather profound and powerful message for a torn sheet of paper.

This exercise would have been very difficult to accomplish if one did not understand the complexities of the Korean history or political situation. Therefore, knowing the ability of the audience to interpret a message is critical. It is for this reason that signs and symbols that are generally known to the public are often used.

CONNOTATION IN ADVERTISING

Businesses and corporations use connotative qualifiers to promote their image via advertising as well. In the ad below, the denotative elements are a male dressed in a coat, holding a fire helmet, with a fire truck in the background, some text, and a small Ford logo in the lower right corner. Connotatively, the image of the fireman often evokes feelings of safety, security, reliability, and dedication.

The text supports this idea as it explains how the man pictured in the ad is a volunteer fireman and emergency medical technician in his community as well as a Ford employee bringing the same level of dedication to others in both aspects of his life. There is no image of a Ford Motor Company product—Ford no longer manufactures larger fire trucks—but the ad is very effective because the connotative qualifiers of safety, security, reliability, and dedication are the type of qualities that Ford would like to have the audience attribute to them.

Courtesy Ford Motor Company, Global Brand Licensing

◉ TRADEMARKS AND PICTOGRAPHS

Trademarks and pictographs are some of the most obvious symbols used in our society. Both groups of symbols are highly functional, and while some are more literal than others, they all must be learned. These small but powerful graphic achievements are complex symbols that can signify corporate recognition and image, or a variety of objects and concepts.

TRADEMARKS CREATE A UNIQUE BRAND IDENTITY

A trademark is a distinctive symbol using a unique typeface and/or graphic element to create an emblem or logo that distinguishes a company, organization, or institution from another. These symbols are intellectual property, and may be legally registered with the U.S. Patent and Trademark Office, giving the company exclusive rights to their use. The use of a distinctive symbol creates immediate recognition and helps to create brand identity for a company or its product, by distinguishing their product from similar products. The recognition of the mark or logo should trigger an image for the consumer of the unique "personality" of that company or product and the goal is to achieve positive connotative qualifiers such as quality and reliability. Therefore, the logo creates a connotative image or mental impression in the mind of the consumer.

Because trademarks enhance the packaging of consumer goods and products, and are also displayed in their subsequent advertising, the public is exposed to countless corporate symbols on a regular basis. This exposure has trained us to identify thousands of these distinguishing marks and even young children are capable of reliably identifying an extensive number of logos.[5] The successful marketing and global reach of some companies have resulted in their trademarks attaining iconic status and recognition worldwide. There are different categories of trademarks and all must be learned through exposure of differing degrees.[6]

Wordmarks

The first category of marks is the wordmark. Using only text, wordmarks are graphic identities that use the complete name of the organization. Because the name is easy to identify this logotype needs the least amount of exposures to introduce to the public and is therefore the most economical. Examples of successful wordmark logos are those of FedEx and Coca-Cola.

In 1994 Federal Express officially adopted "FedEx" as its primary brand.[7] The logo,
created by Lindon Leader, is a wordmark with
a hidden arrow that appears in the negative
space between the "E" and "x" a sign, which
Leader stated in a blog interview signifies "…
speed and precision, both FedEx communicative attributes.[8]

FedEx service marks used by permission

The iconic Coca-Cola script is recognized world wide and has gone
unchanged in the company's lengthy history. It was the bookkeeper of
the creator of the syrup for Coca-Cola who created the name and trademark in distinctive script.[9]

The logos for Disney, Kellogg's, Campbell's, Exxon, Google, and
Yahoo are examples of other wordmarks.

Combination Forms

Combination forms combine the complete name along with a decorative element
such as those found in the Burger King,
Taco Bell, Amazon and Merrill Lynch lo-

Provided courtesy of Frito-Lay North America, Inc.

gos. Both wordmarks and combination forms take little to learn as the
name is clearly indicated and exposures are minimal. The Tostitos logo
is unique as the graphics within it creates two people dipping a gold chip
in a bowl of red salsa, adding a visual representation of the brand.

While the audience needs few exposures to learn this type of mark,
they also can become so accustomed to the visual symbol within the
logo, that in some cases the name can be eliminated leaving just the
symbol. Such was the case with Nike when the company name was
dropped leaving only the trademarked swoosh.

Lettermarks

Lettermarks, the third category of trademarks, use only the initials of
the company name. The representation of these forms must be learned
through greater exposure than the previous two categories and is therefore more expensive to introduce to the public.[10]

In some cases, the true name of the company may rarely be recognized
as is the case with 3M. Interestingly enough their logo has achieved a high
level of recognition and people can name a variety of products that the
company manufactures but they do not know that the actual name of the
company is Minnesota Mining and Manufacturing. [11]

Reprinted with permission of GE.

The logo for GE (General Electric) has achieved a high level of consumer recognition as it can be seen on countless consumer products that enhance the average American home from light bulbs to home appliances.

Other famous lettermarks represent HBO (Home Box Office), IBM (International Business Machines), GMC (General Motors Corporation), and CNN (Cable News Network).

Brandmarks

Brandmarks, are pure symbol and the hardest to learn. These logos must have extensive exposure to learn; therefore, brandmarks are the most costly to introduce to the public. There is, however, a distinct advantage to a brandmark in a global market where translation of the previous textual categories into different languages may prove problematic. A brandmark needs no translation, just recognition through increased exposure.

Increased exposure creates greater awareness and recognition, which the Shell Oil Company and Chevrolet have been able to achieve. Chevy's "bow-tie" logo has achieved a high level of exposure as its parent company GM is one of the largest producers of cars in the world,[12] and the shell used by Shell Oil produces immediate name recognition.

Brandmarks are also used by Apple Computers, Nike, and car manufacturers such as Honda and Mercedes. As previously mentioned, Nike adapted their logo to a brandmark with the swoosh, and AT&T and Target, have also been successful at dropping their name leaving the recognized graphic element to stand alone.

UPDATING THE COMPANY IMAGE AND THE MARK

Because a logo is an important aspect of any company's brand identity and reflects the company's image and mission to the public, corporations understand the need to keep their image fresh to create a perception of being up to date and in touch with their consumers.

Company marks or logos are some of the most recognizable symbols used in the world and must present a positive image of the entity they represent. As discussed, these marks must reflect the company's changing image and mission and are a major component of the brand image. They are meant to produce connotative attributes in the mind of the audience creating a positive perception so that they may feel good about the organization and what it does.

After 80 years, British Petroleum (BP) changed their logo from the dark green shield to a lighter and brighter multi-layered sunburst image using the iconic green and yellow. The resulting connotation of the new logo symbolizes the changes in the companies efforts to move beyond petroleum energy sources and highlights the idea of sustainable energy.[13]

The shield and package of the UPS logo was created in 1961 by renowned designer Paul Rand, and represented the company's primary mission of package delivery. After 42 years, the UPS logo was changed in 2003, eliminating the string-tied package "symbolizing UPS's expansion from package delivery into a broader array of … services." The latest logo is the fourth in the company's 97 years in business.[14]

Many companies change their logo with much greater frequency, refreshing their look with more contemporary typefaces and graphics. One of those companies is Kentucky Fried Chicken (KFC) who has changed their look many times over the years while sustaining the iconic image of its founder Colonel Sanders.[15] Most recently, the company's mark has a more retro look.

Numerous companies, like Apple, Amazon, Wendy's, Pizza Hut, Xerox, and even the Windows operating system are among several organizations who have updated iconic logos, and subsequently their image, as the companies try to reflect the changing nature of their business.

KFC has changed their logo at least six times since 1952 but one thing remains the same - the image of the founder, Colonel Sanders

PICTOGRAPHS ARE OUR HIEROGLYPHS

US Department of Transportation

Pictographs are commonly used visual symbols that represent objects or concepts.

Ideographs and pictographs, are visual symbols that allow us to communicate without the use of written or spoken words. Ideographs are picture symbols that refer to an idea or concept; for example the skull and cross bones has come to represent death. Pictographs represent words, phrases, or objects and many have developed into elaborate symbol systems.

We should not be surprised at the ability to use pictographs as a visual language as man began to communicate in pictorial form. Even the type forms we use today were derived from early pictographs and were refined as civilizations traded more than just their goods and products but also their written language.

Pictographs today are our modern hieroglyphs, having been developed into symbols used as the language of public information. Many of these symbol systems are at use on our roadways, national parks, hospitals, and other public buildings, and at every Olympiad.

One of the first successful systems was created by Viennese philosopher Otto Neurath in the 1920s. Calling his system Isotype (International System of TYpographic Picture Education), his principles remain the basis of international pictographs today.[16]

These symbols are purely denotative, evoking no emotional response. The key to a successful system is to reduce the shape to a simplistic flat silhouette that offers ease of recognition and little ambiguity, eliminate any irrelevant information, use consistency through coordinated objects depicted in a similar style, and the ability to reproduce the symbols in one color.

Road Signs

Standardized road signs, using a system of pictographs, were first introduced in Europe in 1909. Standardized signs in the United States began much later with a formal fed-

eral manual in 1935. A slow evolution of signage developed into the common pictographs used on roadways today, which align more closely with those used around the world.[17]

Transportation Signage

In 1974 the American Institute of Graphic Arts (AIGA) working with the U.S. Department of Transportation (DOT) approved a set of signs for use in transportation centers such as air terminals, rail stations, and other public buildings. The design firm of Cook & Shanosky was given the task to create the symbols. The resulting fifty symbols is now known as *Symbol Signs,* named after the government report detailing their creation.[18]

US Department of Transportation

The Symbol Signs are a series of symbols created specifically for the Department of Transportation to ease travel communication.

The symbols pictured here represent the following concepts: taxi, restaurant, coffee shop, no smoking, telephone, baggage lockers, bar, barber shop, and lost and found.

Olympic Symbols

Every Olympiad creates a communication challenge as athletes, spectators, and media from around the world converge at a foreign site. While the five interlocking rings have been a symbol of the modern Olympic Games since the 1920s, unique signage systems are created for each venue. While many symbol systems have been created for the various Olympic Games, the signage for the 1972 Olympic Games in Munich, Germany were hailed as a "semiotic climax of international

These symbols were created by Otl Aicher for use in the 1972 summer Olympic Games held in Munich, Germany.

© 1976 by ERCO Leuchten GmbH

The 2016 games held in Rio de Janeiro, Brazil used a much more fluid image of the human form along with thinner lines for the features of the sport

pictures."[19] The symbols were such successful international symbols that they were used at the Frankfurt airport and would be reused in the 1976 Montreal games.[20] The key to the success of these symbols was the sophisticated, refined design and clarity in recognition.

Each Olympiad has continued to use similar iconography, though each one has created a unique approach to the stylized symbols used for the sporting events and venues of the games.

Pictographs used for any purpose are pictorial symbols, which have the ability to communicate by crossing language barriers when consistently recognized images are used.

◉ EXPECTATIONS AND MEANING

Clarity in any message is achieved when signs and symbols are used that are more easily recognizable to the public. The simplistic shapes of the figures in the Olympic logos indicated the common actions in the various sporting events. Successful messages are constructed using signs and symbols that are readily identifiable but also understood for their common meaning.

GENERALIZATIONS

For example, the differentiation between good and evil is often cor- related to the colors of white and black. In western films the "good guys" always wore the white hats and the "bad guys" wore black hats. This differentiation occurred out of consideration for the audience who, when watching the early low-contrast black-and-white films, were better able to easily identify the antag- onists and protagonists by the color of their hats.

Generalizations of this nature are used to ease communication and are based on the acquired knowledge and expectations of the audience. In time we learn what labels to attach to objects particularly if they meet certain expectations.

When asked to identify the doctor in the image at upper right, we might expect hesitation as the man and woman do not meet our expectations of a doctor. One might even question whether they were doctors at all. But the second image satisfies those expectations, as we see that both parties wear a stethoscope around their necks and are dressed in scrubs or lab coats. These tools of the trade are our expected visual clues that help us to identify the imagery as it was intended.

While generalizations can make communi- cation easier, there is an inherent danger in this concept as generalizations can lead to stereo- types. These can include gender stereotyping, as one might generalize this last image even further by identifying only the male as the doctor and the female as a nurse.

◉ CONTEXT

Meaning also occurs within a context, or setting. If the environ- ment, or background changes, the meaning may shift entirely. The context allows the audience to gain a frame of reference to perceive meaning based on the contextual relationship.

Without the added context of the silverware in the second image, the simple image of the top image could be any square of fabric.

CHANGING THE CONTEXT

This concept can be demonstrated further by using the image of the napkin which could be misinterpreted as any piece of cloth because we do not see it in a specific context or environment. Once we see the second image, the meaning is clearer as we see the cloth folded in a particular manner and accompanied with silverware that offers greater context.

As the same object is placed into different settings the frame of reference changes and so too does the meaning. Therefore, as this example shows, the context in which an image is placed can affect the message.

CONTEXT AND OMISSIONS

Any constructed message is pieced together to communicate meaning. In the previous examples the meaning of an image changed when the subject, or "text," was placed in a different context or environment. But what happens if there is no context?

Images without Context

In the example at right, a row of tanks are rumbling through a city in formation. Is it an invasion? A parade? Or a military unit on training maneuvers?

Because no context is given, the image is left to the perception of the viewer.

What may look like two people arguing may really be two people in an animated discussion or yelling just to be heard over nearby construction. Interpreting the image below is difficult as the situation is ambiguous. Is this a couple having a disagreement, or just a pensive moment? There are several alternative interpretations leaving an uncertainty about its meaning.

Therefore, without a frame of reference, there is no contextual relationship for one to accurately determine the situation.

While these examples illustrate images lacking or omitting a context, even images within a context are capable of omitting information. Because a camera cannot take in a scene in its entirety, one must be aware that some of the information is omitted.

Ambiguity—These two images offer no context in which to base the circumstances, therefore we are left to ponder several alternate interpretations.

Omissions through Cropping

Any image can be cropped to fit a given space. Care must be taken when cropping an image so as not to change the context of the meaning. This is especially true in photojournalism as cropping out background information to focus in on a subject may restrict the ability of the audience to comprehend the situation without accompanying text, again causing ambiguity in interpretation.

In these examples, the first image appears to be a beautiful waterfront with an alluring sky and enticing water. It looks peaceful enough until the viewpoint is broadened to reveal a beach strewn with garbage that has washed up on the shore, completely destroying the beauty of the scene, and revealing a much different scenario.

The original image at the top has been cropped two different ways.

What do the omissions suggest?

In the examples above one image can be cropped a number of ways, eliminating members of this team of professionals. This can suggest that a smaller team worked on a project or as the lower center image suggests that there were only women involved.

As this chapter indicates, there are many ways in which we have come to learn to interpret messages and many ways in which that interpretation can be hindered. We have been trained to seek meaning in messages and to do so we must learn to recognize the symbolism and connotative meanings in images as well as pictographs used for public communication or corporate identification.

Not enough information or a lack of accumulated knowledge can result in distracting or ambiguous interpretations as we try to fit those perceptions to the given context as well as within our expectations.

CASE IN POINT

DECONSTRUCTION

What do you see?

Start with the basics–what do you see? Break the image down to basic elements being careful to identify the building blocks used to create this image without interpretation.

Use of the Trojan® Warrior Head Logo® and EVOLVE.™ trademarks, and EVOLVE print ad for TROJAN® brand Condoms is with the express written permission of Church & Dwight Co., Inc, Princeton, New Jersey. TROJAN, EVOLVE, and the Warrior Head logo are trademarks of Church & Dwight Virginia Co., Inc.
© Church & Dwight Virginia Co., Inc. 2007.

Identifying basic elements

This ad has a number of pigs sitting at tables and on stools, they have beverages and electronic devices, and there are also five human forms–four female and one male. The dimly lit room has a counter running across it with shelves behind it and along the back wall filled with bottles of different shapes. There is text running along the bottom that states "evolve. be a man. use a condom every time. nobody likes a pig." The Trojan name and logo are also included.

It isn't easy to merely state the obvious–the basic elements–because we are trained to interpret but once we identify the basic elements in a piece we can start applying meaning. Notice we didn't automatically state that there are pigs in a bar

What are the connotative meanings?

As the analysis continues, we can systematically add implied or connotative meaning.

The room appears to be a bar with pigs as the primary customers. Yes, pigs in a bar drinking what appears to be beer and other alcoholic beverages. Certainly this is a bit unusual and is a significant approach to capture the initial attention of the audience.

So why the pigs? An alternative definition for a pig is a person who is found to be dirty, repulsive, unpleasant, or self-centered. The pigs in this case are a metaphor for men who do not use condoms, suggesting that they are self-serving in their lack of concern for their female partner.

The idea of a pig, or in this case the inconsiderate male, is evidenced by the expressions on the faces of the females who are sitting with the pigs. They certainly appear to be repulsed by the companionship of the pigs.

In comparison, there is a lone human male. So, in a room full of pigs, why is he different? The suggestion is that he is carrying a Trojan condom; he has therefore evolved and is not an inconsiderate pig. But there is more in the imagery that suggests that this male has evolved. He is engaged in conversation with one of the females who appears to find him appealing. Both are smiling, the woman is leaning in towards the male, her hand on his torso, and their faces are intimately close. The act of seduction has been established.

The contrast between this couple and the others is intensified by the visual distinction of the male in white, within the darkened room. While the visual contrast creates attention, it is further exaggerated by what appears to be a spotlight effect. The idea of wearing white amid others in black harkens back to the old western films where the "good guys" wore white hats while the "bad guys" wore black. Therefore, the connotation is that he is a good guy, again, the evolved male. It appears that she found "the one" in a room full of pigs.

These are all strategic choices made in the design of this piece, which contribute to the overall meaning of the message as well as its ability to attract the attention of the audience.

● CONCEPT CHECKLIST

text	context
construction	deconstruction
signs/symbols	semiotics
denotation	connotation
trademark	consensual agreement
acquired knowledge	pictograph

● SUMMARY

- Media messages are texts that we learn to "read."

- Media messages are creations of people who work behind the scenes.

- Media texts are strategically constructed.

- Messages may be packaged as entertainment, information, education, advertising, and persuasion.

- Any message can be deconstructed.

- Semiotics is the study of signs and symbols.

- Images are a collection of signs and symbols

- Images have both denotational and connotational meaning.

- The interpretation of signs are subjective—based on values, expectations, past experience.

- Signs often meet common expectations for effective communication.

- Meaning is achieved through acquired social knowledge and consensual agreement.

- Images are capable of expressing complex ideas.

- Images are placed within a specific context to create the desired meaning

- Omitted information can change the meaning of a message.

- Pictographs and trademarks are the most obvious symbols used in our society.

- Pictographs and trademarks must be learned.

◉ ACTIVITIES

1. Play a game of Pictionary™. See if you can draw the words so that others can identify them. How hard is it to convey certain concepts? Does it help to put the words clues in a context?

2. Choose an image from a magazine, newspaper, or online source without text. What do you think is happening? What is the context? How does context create meaning?

3. Choose an advertisement from a magazine. Identify the elements (signs) used in the advertising image and explain their connotative meaning.

4. There are a number of online apps with logo quizzes. See how many you can identify accurately. Then examine the signs and symbols used to create this identities. How do they represent the company or organization?

5. Take a look at a visual time line behind many company logos. There are websites like these that include a variety of logos from companies in several different industries. Check out https://logos.fandom.com/wiki/Logopedia or https://1000logos.net/

6. We took a quick look at the *Symbol Signs* used by the Department of Transportation. Keep track of the pictographs that you come in contact with. Where were they located? What did they convey?

7. What makes a hero? Who are the heroes of your generation? Why? Ask your parents and grandparents who the heroes of their generations were and why? What character traits did they have? Are there similarities or differences between the generations?

⦿ RESOURCES

Roland Barthes

http://www.academia.edu/5991199/Elements_of_Semiology_Roland_
Barthes_1964

Elements of Semiology, 1964, was originally published by Hill and Wang in 1968 but the first half of the book is reproduced at the above website.

Daniel Chandler

http://www.visual-memory.co.uk/daniel/Documents/S4B/

The website above is an online version of his signature book, Semiotics: The Basics. Chandler is a lecturer in Media and Communication Studies in the Department of Theater, Film, and Television Studies at Aberystwyth University and is also the author of numerous articles on semiotics in advertising which can be acquired through academic databases and Google Scholar.

⦿ ENDNOTES

1. Arthur Asa Berger, Seeing is Believing: An Introduction to Visual Communication, 3rd ed. (New York: McGraw-Hill, 2008), 1

2. Roland Barthes, Elements of Seminology. (New York: Hill and Wang, 1964).

3. Ibid.

4. Ibid

5. P. M. Fischer, M. P. Schwartz, J. W. Richards Jr, A. O. Goldstein and T. H. Rojas, "Brand Logo Recognition by Children Aged 3 To 6 Years. Mickey Mouse and Old Joe the Camel," Journal of the American Medical Association, 266, no. 22 (December 11, 1991).

6. Gregg Berryman, Notes on Graphic Design and Visual Communication, "Marks," (Menlo Park, CA: Crisp Publications, Inc., 1990), 10.

7. "FedEx History." FedEx, 2020, www.fedex.com/en-us/about/history.html.

8. "The Man Behind the FedEx Logo," The Sneeze, <http://www.thesneeze.com/mt-archives/cat_secrets_of_the_fedex_logo.php>.

9. "The Birth of a Refreshing Idea." News & Articles, 2020, www.coca-colacompany.com/company/history/the-birth-of-a-refreshing-idea.

10. Berryman, Notes on Graphic Design, p. 11.

11. "3M History," 3M Corporate web site <https://www.3m.com/3M/en_US/company-us/about-3m/history//> April 2020.

12. "Chevy Logo, Chevrolet Car Symbol Meaning and History." Car Brand Names.com, 20 June 2020, www.car-brand-names.com/chevrolet-logo/.

13. "The BP Brand," BP corporate website, <https://www bp.com/en/global/corporate/who-we-are/our-brands/the-bp-brand.html> June 2020

14. The history of UPS and its logo was compiled from several sources including: Fact Sheet Details, pressroom.ups.com/pressroom/ContentDetailsViewer.page?ConceptType=FactSheets and "UPS." Logopedia, logos.fandom.com/wiki/UPS.

15. The history of KFC and its logo was compiled from several sources including KFC, 2020, global.kfc.com/asset-library/ and "KFC Logo." 1000 Logos The Famous Brands and Company Logos in the World KFC Logo Comments, 1000logos.net/kfc-logo/.

16. Andrew Piemmons Pratt, "It Takes a Story to Tell a Language: The Grammar of Images and the Elements of Language" in Paul Zelevansky's Book of Tales, review of Book of Tales, by Paul Zelevansky, Modern Visual Poetry, December 13, 2005, 2.

17. *"Manual on Uniform Traffic Control Devices"* (MUTCD), U.S. Department of Transportation, Federal Highway Administration < http://mutcd.fhwa.dot.gov/> May 2020.

18. *"Symbol Signs"*, Society and Environment, American Institute of Graphic Arts (AIGA) website < http://www.aiga.org/content.cfm/symbol-signs> April 2020.

19. Ellen Lupton and Abbott Miller,, "Modern Hieroglyphics," *Design Writing Research* (London: Phaidon Press Limited, 1999), 43.

20. Stinson, Liz. "Decoding the Hidden Meanings of Olympic Symbols." Wired, Conde Nast, 3 June 2017, www.wired.com/2016/08/decoding-hidden-meanings-olympic-symbols/.

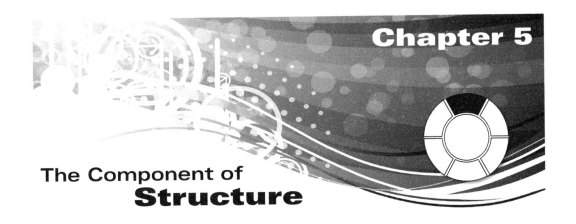

The Component of
Structure

Chapter Objectives

- Describe the five canons of rhetoric.
- Explain the importance of identifying the target audience.
- Recognize the key concepts of invention.
- Recognize the key concepts of arrangement.
- Categorize the visual style and manner of delivery of media messages.
- Distinguish how media messages impact audiences by triggering memories.
- Analyze how media messages are created and interpreted using stored data.

Key Media Literacy Concept #2:
Media messages are structured within a distinct structure or framework.

Key Media Literacy Question #2:
Who is the target audience and how was the message tailored to them?

. . . .

◉ MEDIA AND RHETORIC

As the last chapter demonstrated, media messages are constructed with great care as to meaning and context. While media messages may seem arbitrary and indiscriminate in their construction, they are just the opposite, being carefully crafted with a distinct methodology and structure. Creating media messages can be viewed as artful problem solving where a justifiable argument is carefully arranged to inform or influence an audience. Media messages are, therefore, a form of rhetoric.

Rhetoric is defined as the art of effective communication used to persuade or influence others. Media messages may take a variety of different forms, from a television or radio newscast, a recorded song, a web ad, or a magazine advertisement. The newscast may inform us of a particular issue and why it may be of concern, but it may also persuade the audience to act or get involved. The magazine ad may inform us of a new product, but also persuade us to purchase it. Media messages are packaged as information, entertainment, education, and persuasion. These skillfully crafted messages use a methodology to get a point across to an audience. Exploring the methods or procedures for creating a message will reveal the structure of the message, and being familiar with the principles of rhetoric will help guide this portion of our examination of media literacy. The basis for this strategy can be found in Aristotle's principles of rhetoric.

● ARISTOTLE'S PRINCIPLES OF RHETORIC

Aristotle was a Greek philosopher who studied under the great philosopher Plato. Becoming an educator, like his master, he was credited with opening an academy outside of Athens and later tutoring Alexander the Great.[1] Aristotle understood that speech was a great skill and recognized that there were distinct elements that were inherently present in effective persuasive speeches. Over 2,300 years ago, Aristotle outlined several principles for effective communication and persuasion in his lectures, which were chronicled through his students lecture notes in the book *The Rhetoric*.[2]

The Rhetoric details the various kinds of speeches and the means to construct them. Aristotle believed that an argument was constructed using three components or *artistic proofs*—ethos, logos, and pathos.[3] Ethos is the need to build a sense of credibility for both the messenger and the message, logos is the underlying logic or reasoning that is offered to justify the message, and pathos is the emotional appeal that is made to the audience.

Over 2,300 years ago Aristotle developed a framework for effective communication, which is equally effective today.

Along with these three principles, Aristotle alludes to additional guidelines that would serve as a foundation for rhetorical structure which would be further developed by other orators. Often, it is the Roman orator Cicero who is credited with detailing the five principles, or standards, for effective communication known as the canons of rhetoric: invention, arrangement, style, delivery, and memory.[4]

KEY CONCEPT - FIVE CANONS OF RHETORIC
CREATING THE MEDIA STRUCTURE

The five canons of rhetoric are a key concept of communication that are normally relegated to communication theory or rhetorical criticism classes. While creators of media messages may not be formally taught the structure of the canons per se, they are certainly taught the concepts behind them. Because media design is a deliberate construction, any well planned message will implement this strategy via any given medium. The canons of rhetoric become both the methodology for the creation of messages and the structure or foundation on which they are constructed, and are therefore imperative for the study of media literacy.

Every message should attract the attention of the target audience, be deliberately crafted for that audience, be justified, be delivered in a form that is both appealing and strategically placed in the media, and leave an impression on the audience.

Invention   Arrangement   Style   Delivery   Memory

THE CANON OF INVENTION

Invention, as per the canons of rhetoric, is the construction of a persuasive argument through reasoning and rationale. An argument in this sense is the topic or subject matter of the message, which is then explained through rationalization by offering proof or justification to support it. In essence, information is presented and justified in a manner reasonable for the audience. The core of invention is identifying what the information is and to whom is it being presented.

The Importance of Defining the Target Audience

Identification of the target audience is an essential element of invention. A message can be specifically tailored to appeal to the needs, concerns, or desires of that audience. Determining a target audience is a science in and of itself, usually involving market research to identify a specific audience through statistical data. A population, or audience, can be defined through various characteristics.

Demographics identifies certain variables such as age, gender, marital status, employment, income, education level, ethnicity, and even home and vehicle ownership.

An audience can be further defined through psychographics, where the behaviors, attitudes, and opinions of an audience are identified and geographics determines the location of the audience.

These variables are important considerations when constructing a message. Men may perceive a message differently from women. The concerns of an older generation may be different from the younger generation, renters and homeowners would have different concerns, while one's interests and personality may determine the kind of vehicle that they drive, and where one lives may determine various seasonal needs. For example, someone living in the Northeast would have a greater need for warm clothing like parkas, gloves, and hats as well as snow removal equipment such as shovels or snowblowers. An individual who likes the outdoors may be interested in camping equipment, and perhaps a vehicle that would not only be large enough to transport the equipment, but have the ability to travel over rugged terrain.

Invention, therefore, is the identification of the target audience so the message can be tailored to them, and the use of logical rationale to appeal to the needs, concerns, or desires of that audience.

Building credibility with an audience, or *ethos*, is another of Aristotle's artistic proofs of rhetoric.[5] If an audience feels that the source of the message is credible, they are more apt to believe the message. If the messenger can connect with an audience, or seems to have achieved a level of expertise, then the message is better received. This is often seen in news programs, talk shows, and commercials where experts, celebrities, and others who have shared an experience are interviewed or used to sell a product or to weigh in on an issue. These techniques will be discussed further in the next chapter.

Developing an Argument

The subject matter of media messages today vary widely as a news story may want us to be aware of or consider an issue of public importance, while an advertisement may try to persuade us to purchase a product. Whatever form the message takes, there is an intention or purpose for that message, as well as the means to justify it.

It is while crafting the message that Aristotle's artistic proof of *logos* is employed. The creator of a message must employ logic or reasoning to back up their claim.[6] For instance, if one were to make a statement such as,"there is no reason for anyone to attend college," there would be a call for that person to explain the reasoning behind their statement. In media, we must consider the purpose of the message, such as the topic of a news story or the product in an advertisement, but also how that message is justified to the audience. We can look at how that news story is formulated to identify the reasons to bring the subject to our attention, and why it should concern or will affect the audience. We could evaluate an advertisement for the product attributes that may be beneficial to the audience.

The purpose of advertising is to create an awareness and a desire in the consumer. The argument, or topic of the ad, is to promote the product or service by rationalizing the value to the audience. Often this is done by evaluating the features, characteristics, and product attributes. In the Dodge Caravan ad below, the audience is enticed with a variety of visual symbols and accompanying text extolling the many attributes of the vehicle. One can see that the many layers of paint and top coats prevent chipping, that the vehicle has anti-lock brakes, a tight turning radius, compartments for maps, facial tissues, a keyless entry system, sliding doors that remain open even when parked on an incline, and the tape measure signifies a spacious interior.

Courtesy Chrysler LLC

Advertising imagery or text that explores the product features and characteristics is one method in justifying the product to an audience.

While the product attributes in the Caravan ad are fairly obvious, a subtle approach can be equally effective, as in the Ford Motor Company ad discussed in the previous chapter. The connotative attributes of safety, security, and reliability that are implied by the fireman are the same qualities that Ford would like to have the audience attribute to them

THE CANON OF ARRANGEMENT

Arrangement deals with how a message is organized. Aristotle expressed the need for a well-organized message with an introduction that would capture the audience's attention, a body that raises points to justify the purpose, and a conclusion that summarizes the message for the audience. Media messages are created in a similar manner. Designers arrange messages using the elements and principles of design as their principal building blocks. These elements are arranged using a visual hierarchy where visual information is prioritized by creating a focal point to attract the audience's attention, continuing with secondary information, tertiary information, etc. Similarly film, television, and radio must follow a sequence, or order of events, for the audience to follow a story line.

Analyzing the arrangement of a message will illustrate the methodology used in its construction to prioritize the information with a visual hierarchy.

Order guides the layout, and can be easily identified in the example of a simple poster design. This might start with what is meant to capture the audience's attention or the focal point. Here, the large graphic at the top is the focal point followed by the rest of the hierarchy; the bold headline, followed by a defining subtitle; then a secondary image; and finally the detailed body copy.

A visual hierarchy begins with a focal point to draw attention to the piece, then a secondary object, a tertiary object, etc. Text and images must be arranged on a page to attract our attention and entice us to read.

Big Headline Here
a smaller subhead

By emphasizing an element on the page, the designer creates a point of entry, drawing the audiences attention into the piece. The remaining visual information is arranged and ordered in such a way to draw the eye through the piece.

In Western cultures, printed information is generally read from top to bottom and from left to right. Therefore, the audience usually starts at the top left corner and works their way down through a piece, unless the designer has created a focal point elsewhere on the page, and offers us another way to flow through it.

The elements of design are the basic components, or objects, that are arranged to create the layout and are identified as: line, shape, texture, space, size, color, and contrast. These are used in combination with each other to create a composition.[7]

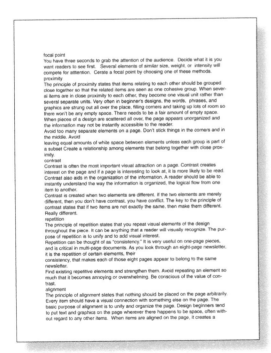

If the text was left in its raw state, as in the example at left, we would find the bland text boring and indistinguishable from other pages. When creating a visual hierarchy by adding graphic elements to create a focal point, categorizing the information, and arranging the text in a neat and legible manner, the page becomes more interesting and more useful.

 **KEY CONCEPTS - CREATING THE STRUCTURE**
ELEMENTS AND PRINCIPLES OF DESIGN

The elements of design are the basic components or objects that are arranged to create the layout and are identified as: line, shape, texture, space, size, color, and contrast. These are used in combination with each other to create a composition.

The principles of design—balance, emphasis, rhythm, and unity—describe how the elements are arranged.

ELEMENTS OF DESIGN	PRINCIPLES OF DESIGN
Line	Balance
Shape	Rhythm
Texture	Emphasis
Size	Unity
Space	
Color	
Contrast	

Line

A line is the path between points, and may be thick, thin, curved, or straight.

Here lines of varying thicknesses are used to illustrate the shape, and details, of this car. This dramatic approach is highlighted even further with what appears to be a reflection below it.

The contrast of the black background adds to the effect.

Drink. Drive. Spill.   *Party sober and drug free.*

Copyright © Craig Frazier. Reprinted with permission.

Musical Arts Center

Courtesy Musical Arts Center

Shape

Shape is a closed form such as a rectangle, circle, or triangle. Our eye is drawn to the large black shape in the poster, the focal point of the piece. This shape has the texture of an asphalt road with the dashed dividing line. The form represents a skull, and, as we noted in the previous chapter, a skull often symbolizes death.

The secondary information in the visual hierarchy is represented by the shape depicting a bottle spilling its contents onto the roadway. The tertiary information, or third level of information, is the text at the bottom that informs the reader of the dangers of drinking and driving.

Texture

Texture is the appearance of a surface that can be rough or smooth, and in a print piece can be designed to be visually perceived as dimensional. The analysis of the above example denoted a roadway surface in the shape of the skull.

The poster for the Musical Arts Center, at left, depicts a maple leaf with a gradation of tone created via a stippling effect with small dots giving a textural quality to the surface.

The maple leaf is the focal point of the piece, while the lines depicting the musical staff are the secondary information, and the text at the bottom is the tertiary information. This poster is an example of how elements of design can be layered as it uses the elements discussed thus far: line, shape, and texture.

Space

In two-dimensional pieces, space is relational and can be described as the area in or around things, positive and negative space, and dimensional space.

A creative example of the use of positive and negative space occurs  with this one million logo, using the shapes that are created in the negative space in and around each letter. At first glance, we see only the various shapes. Eventually, we realize that we have to look beyond the shapes and the letterforms are then revealed, making for a more unusual and striking design than using the solid letterforms themselves.

Reviewing the drunk driving poster, on page 87, we have a prime example of negative space used to create emphasis. The empty space around the elements allows the skull and bottle to become more prominent. Not only does negative space, allow for the emphasis of elements, it is also aesthetically pleasing and gives the eye a resting place.

Another element is the spacial relationship of objects that allows for dimensional space or the illusion of depth. From past experience, we know that items in the foreground appear larger, and often overlap, those items in the background.

The example below is evidence of this, as the male is perceived to be in the foreground as he is larger, with the woman in the background.

This image also uses negative space as the far left portion of the image is blank–with the male as the main point of emphasis in the middle, and the woman at right–a photographic technique known as the rule of thirds. Notice how the barbell the male is holding also points to the woman, acting as a directional element. Both techniques will be discussed in a later chapter.

Size

Size is the overall dimension of something, simply how big or small something is. In the example at left, the dog is the largest and most prominent item in the page, and clearly the focal point.

Color

Color can help communicate ideas, as with the traffic light discussed in an earlier chapter; we recognize that green means go and red means stop.

Color can also be used to express emotions and to create emphasis. Warm colors (red, orange, and yellow) are more dominant; therefore, they "shout" in contrast to the cool colors (blue, green, and purple), which recede or "whisper."

While there are many different characteristics to color theory, a few of the basic terms will be covered for simplicity. Color palettes can be created using the color wheel to identify relational schemes. Complementary colors are those opposite each other on the color wheel, analogous colors are those next to each other, and triadic palettes are created with three colors equidistant from each other on the color wheel.

The three primary colors are yellow, red and blue and their compliments–orange, violet, and green–are known as the secondary color palette. The tertiary palette are those between the primary and secondary colors and are blends of the two, yellow orange for example. Color images can be found online.

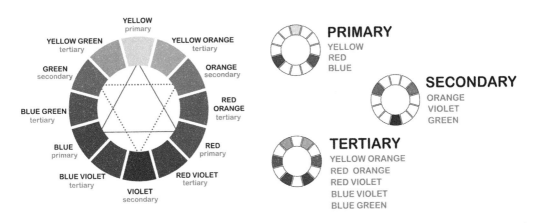

Basic color palettes—primary, secondary, tertiary

Copyright © Denver Department of Health & Hospitals. Reprinted with permission.

Contrast

Contrast is also known as value, and is best described as how light or dark something is. Often contrast is created by placing light and dark subjects together to create or accentuate their differences. The example above is striking not only for the subject matter, but also because the image begins as pure white, through the graduation of tone in the child's face, and into pure black. The contrast is stark and representative of the loss of innocence, the despair, and the stigma of child abuse.

Balance

Balance is the distribution of weight, and may be symmetrical with an even distribution of weight, or asymmetrical with an uneven distribution of weight. In the first example, weight is distributed evenly; therefore, this is an example of symmetrical balance, and the second example is asymmetrical.

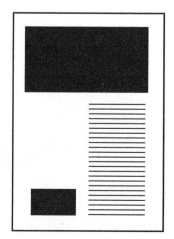

Copyright © 2008 Morla Design, Inc.

Rhythm

Rhythm is the perception of movement through pattern or repetition. The example at left is evidence of a variety of pattern, including the pattern of lines that radiate from the building, the textural pattern between the lines, the boxes in the corners, the pattern on the building, and even the textual elements at the top and bottom of the poster.

Emphasis

Emphasis is the dominant element of a piece, essentially the focal point, and the top level of the visual hierarchy. Emphasis can be created through size, contrast, and color.

The eye is drawn to the young girl's face in the poster on the previous page due to contrast, and the leaf, skull, and dog in the posters in the preceding pages because of size and contrast, and to the building in the poster to the left for the same reasons.

Unity

Unity is achieved when similar elements are used in a work to create a continuity or sameness throughout.

At left, are a unified series of icons representing various educational concepts. The images are similar in that they are depicted using only a linear style without shading.

The graphics, circular patterns, and typeface used within this book are placed in a unified fashion at the beginning of each chapter and are used similarly throughout the book.

Same subject, different styles—The floral images shown here, one illustrative and one photographic, have a different quality to them.

THE CANON OF STYLE

Style involves the aesthetic or artistic choices made in the creation of a message. Strategic choices are made about the imagery, text, music or other audio used. In our visual world, how the imagery in a piece is created has much to do with setting a tone or mood for the message, whether it is a formal or informal approach, or uses illustrative or photographic imagery, and other production elements such as color and type.

Another aspect to creating an artful message is to distinguish the underlying aesthetics through a shared technique or appearance. Simply put, one should look at a piece to see if it has a distinctive style in its appearance, using references from a specific era, or culture, follows a trend, or uses a specific technique.

Analyzing Style

The ability to analyze style is often dependent on a broad base of accumulated knowledge in order to recognize different art forms, historical periods, cultural influences, or techniques. Although audiences can't always pinpoint a technique specifically, they often recognize a familiarity in the approach.

Aside from cultural influences, style can be defined by historical periods, such as the Victorian era or the Gothic period. Artistic groups share a common technique such as the Impressionists, and art forms created in specific geographic locales had a distinct style like that of the Byzantines. DaVinci's *Mona Lisa* or Michelangelo's statue of *David* are classic in their approach, with a heightened sense of realism and harmony, while contemporary art abstracted forms in a more streamlined and angular manner.

Because there are a number of creative approaches that can be used to carry out a message, a more extensive analysis will be undertaken by devoting another component, and therefore another chapter of this book, to the creative approaches used in messages.

Color Can Reflect Emotions

As stated earlier, color can reflect a variety of emotions and develop the mood or tone of a piece. Red can represent a wide gamut of emotions from love to hate, while green can represent envy, yellow happiness, and blue sadness or peacefulness. At the same time, color can represent concepts as red connotes danger or evil, green-growth, yellow-sunshine, and blue-water or sky.

The color of an image can be adjusted to reflect these moods or concepts,. Images can be altered through software programs that can add filters, adjust color channels, or produce a number of special effects.

Even choosing to eliminate color by opting for a black and white image is a strategic choice. This approach can create a classically elegant image or set a particular tone, as in the child abuse poster mentioned previously. This poster would not have worked as well in color, in fact we would have been distracted by the color, and the connotation of darkness would not have been as impactful.

Type Sets the Tone

Typography is the selection, arrangement, or use of type. Textual information is usually a significant element of print pieces, as a lot of information can be disseminated in a small amount of space. Arranging this textual information is a careful and deliberate act of any well

The top image above, reflects a more elegant or classic style, while the lower images represent a retro or nostalgic style.

designed piece. Careful crafting of a message ensures a visual hierarchy of information, as well as readability and legibility. There is a skill in designing with type as typefaces should be combined with great care and discretion. We have probably all seen the flyer, newsletter, or presentation where the creator used a multitude of typefaces from the font menu because they thought they were "cool," but instead was hard to read and amateurish. While entire classes are devoted to the study of typography, a short overview of the subject can aid in making deliberate choices when producing a piece, as well as to evaluate with enhanced knowledge.

Type can also reflect the mood or tone of a piece; therefore, the selection of type is also strategic to the piece. Certain typefaces are more appropriate for specific uses, and some reflect a specific style. Take the examples below, some are more formal than others, some much more casual. Example #3 has a western style to it while #5 is reminiscent of the Art Nouveau movement.

The choice of type must reflect the purpose and expectations of the piece. Example #6 may not be appropriate for a corporate annual report, but we might expect to see a typeface of this nature in a formal invitation.

⦿ **SAMPLE TYPEFACES**

1. Media Literacy
2. **Media Literacy**
3. MEDIA LITERACY
4. MEDIA LITERACY
5. Media Literacy
6. *Media Literacy*

There are several categories of type to choose from. Example #1 is a serif typeface. This category is easily recognized by the slight projections that finish the stroke of the letterforms, the "feet" that they stand on. Serif typefaces are very readable and are most commonly used for the body text of most newspapers, magazines, and books.

Example #2 is a sans serif typeface. There are no serifs; sans is the French word for without. Therefore these typefaces are "without serifs." The narrow letters, with optically equal strokes, are more contemporary and easily read.

Example #6 is a script designed to resemble handwriting. It is not suitable for body copy, as it is difficult to read in longer line lengths. There are a wide variety of scripts that can be either formal or informal.

Novelty typefaces vary widely and are visually distinctive and meant to attract attention. Examples #3 and #5 are examples of novelty typefaces. They can stimulate various connotative meanings, are unsuitable for body text, and are best when used sparingly.

A typeface can also vary by weight and style; a bold typeface is a scream compared to the whisper of the light typeface, and the condensed version can squeeze more type into a space.

Typeface choice is an important part of the design and should both support and enhance the style of the design.

THE CANON OF DELIVERY

Style and delivery are entwined as both involve the aesthetic choices made in the creation of the piece. Style is the method of expression, including the aesthetic choices made, while delivery concentrates on how those aesthetic choices are carried out or the manner in which the message is presented.

Eventually, the final form must be decided upon - a news story may be prepared for broadcast, print, or the web, while ad campaigns will include advertisements for multiple formats such as TV and radio, magazines, and online. The film industry not only produces the films but also the trailers and posters, as well as social media campaigns, to promote them.

Ultimately, how a piece is rendered and what form it takes are the primary objectives.

⦿ IMAGERY FALLS ON A CONTINUUM
FROM REALISM THROUGH ABSTRACTION TO ICON

Images can be rendered in a number of ways. The examples shown here illustrate the various approaches that exist along the continuum. Starting with the most realistic image, a photograph, then a realistic drawing, down through various forms of abstraction, and ending with the pure symbol.

Imagery Falls on a Continuum

When creating imagery for media messages, there are a vast number of considerations to make, among them how a message is rendered and the level of representation to be used. First, there is the choice to use either an illustration or a photographic image. Illustrative images can use a variety of techniques creating a more formal or realistic image or a more stylized or informal approach. The images shown on the previous page all artistically depict lighthouses, yet all are very different in their approach. Some are more primitive in the manner in which they were rendered, while some are more true to life; yet nothing is as realistic as a photograph.

The representation of an object falls on a continuum from realism, through various stages of stylization, ending in symbolism. The most realistic approach would be to use a photograph followed by a realistic drawing or painting. Various states of stylization follow as the object becomes more abstract through the reduction of various visual factors, culminating in pure symbolism where ultimate simplicity is achieved, much like that of a pictograph. As with a pictograph, these symbols must be learned, as they are reduced to rather simplistic forms.

THE CANON OF MEMORY

The last canon of rhetoric was added later by Roman rhetoricians recognizing the strength of Aristotle's theory. Before teleprompters, speeches were committed to memory, but equally important was for any speaker to touch their audience enough to walk away with something memorable. This is where we place emphasis in today's communication—making communication memorable.

This is especially important in a world abundant with messages. From the 24 hour news cycle, push messages from our apps, text messages, and email we are inundated with constant updates and communication. Add to this the sheer amount of messages within each of these forms and it is even more important to cut through the clutter of all of messages.

Take for instance a magazine or newspaper, the number of ads is often equal to, or more than, the editorial content. Finding ways to be more creative help certain ads stand out from the profusion of advertising. Attention getting headlines, and teasers, help news media entice audiences and readers to their broadcasts and websites.

Once the attention of the audience is achieved it is equally important to impact that audience by creating an impression on them. If the audience leaves the movie theater moved by what they have seen—whether it be to tears or laughter—they will talk to friends about the film perhaps enticing others to attend. A television commercial or magazine ad will only be effective if the audience is aware of a product enough to recognize it in the store, or, better yet, to seek the product out.

Unusual Images Are Memorable

As stated, there are a variety of ways to make a message memorable. One method is to use an unusual image, or an image in an unusual way, so that it stands out from the rest or "cuts through the clutter" of the vast number of media messages bombarding audiences through the assorted forms of media.

Because unusual images attract more attention and become more noticeable among the jumble of media messages, they are apt to have a greater impact on the audience and become more memorable. These images also have a tendency to become more interactive as more time is spent interpreting the message.

Schema Theory

Another aspect of memory is the ability to use our stored data or accumulated knowledge and experiences—in other words our memory—to make sense of what we see in mediated messages.

Schema theory, developed by R. C. Anderson, states that our accumulated knowledge is organized in such a way as to exist in a complex system that acts as a reference library.[8] Simply stated, an individual's stored cache of data is like a file cabinet where individual files are pulled to interpret messages and are even cross-referenced to complete ideas or evaluations.

Essentially we pull the files from our mental file cabinet to interpret messages, pulling multiple files, if needed, particularly with unusual images, and creating new files, as we gain further knowledge.

For example, the image pictured here appears to be that of a morphed cat woman. The image was interpreted by pulling files for "cat" and "woman." Our cross-referencing tells us that this cannot actually take place because this kind of fantastical being does not exist. The result is a new file.

KEY CONCEPTS - SCHEMA THEORY
USING OUR ACCUMULATED KNOWLEDGE

Schema theory describes our patterns to organize accumulated knowledge to provide a framework for future understanding in order to interpret information, make sense of contradictions and file that new information. There are several principles to schema theory:

1. General knowledge and concepts must be taught and are stored in a meaningful manner.
2. Connections are made between ideas in a manner similar to cross-referencing information.
3. Knowledge continues to accumulate particularly as we age and gain more experience sometimes restructuring our references (schemata).
4. Prior knowledge is necessary for new knowledge to occur.[9]

Triggering Memories

The final aspect of making messages memorable is the ability to trigger memories in the audience. Appealing to the audience's emotions, or *pathos*, is the third of Aristotle's artistic proofs. This appeal strategy can be quite effective in persuading an audience.[10]

Connecting to an audience on an emotional level is important at any stage whether it is to create positive brand recognition like the Ford ad, on page 59, connecting them to an issue or concern, or to a product

using favorable memories like a bonfire at camp or a gathering of family or neighborhood friends under a starlit sky sharing stories and roasted marshmallows.

A variety of emotions can be used as creative approaches, which can include positive emotions such as kindness or affection but can also include fear.

Emotional approaches are just one of the many appeal strategies that can be used in mediated messages, and as there are so many they will be discussed at length in the next chapter.

◉ CASE IN POINT
ANALYZING STRUCTURE

Using the canons of rhetoric as a basis for analysis the advertisement below can be deconstructed to determine the underlying structure or framework.

Use of the Trojan® Warrior Head Logo® and EVOLVE.™ trademarks, and EVOLVE print ad for TROJAN® brand Condoms is with the express written permission of Church & Dwight Co., Inc, Princeton, New Jersey. TROJAN, EVOLVE, and the Warrior Head logo are trademarks of Church & Dwight Virginia Co., Inc. © Church & Dwight Virginia Co., Inc. 2007.

Target Audience

The bar, with a roomful of singles–even if they are pigs–suggests that the target audience is single men and women, 25-35 years old, potentially young professionals, becoming established in their careers, and are looking for a committed relationship.

Invention

The premise of the message is that those that are sexually active, in this case primarily males, need to be responsible and use condoms. The rationale is that as men and women begin the game of courtship, some will be considerate and careful, and some will not. It is evident that the lone male human is different in some way. Dressed in white, the connotation is that he is also one of the "good guys," the evolved and considerate male. The pigs are a metaphor for the inconsiderate, self-serving male with little concern for their partners.

Arrangement

The visual hierarchy begins with the focal point. In this dark image, the eye gravitates toward the brightest item on the page–the couple with the male dressed in white. The secondary item, is the cluster of pigs with another female to the left. The hierarchy continues as it cascades down the page eventually to the pigs in the foreground, ending with the tagline at the bottom.

Style

The aesthetic choices are dominated by the contrast of the dark bar and the spotlit couple. The contrast and spotlight effect create a point of emphasis. The spatial relationship of the clusters of pigs creates movement from the highlighted couple in the background and eventually to the pigs sitting center foreground.

Delivery

The image of a bar full of pigs as clientele is a seemingly realistic photograph, though we know it is not possible. Therefore, it is somewhat stylized, a photo illustration, using digital manipulation. Again, the use of the contrast of black and white is strategic to the connotative meaning of the message.

Memory

This piece uses an unusual piece of imagery which tends to be more memorable, attract more attention, and have greater audience impact. We must use our previous knowledge to understand the connotative nuances occurring in the image, starting with the metaphorical pigs. We need to have a prior understanding of what it means to "be a pig," again, as someone who is repulsive, unpleasant, or self-centered. Furthermore, we have to understand the meaning behind the black versus white correlation to good versus evil. These ideas are filed away in our schema, that common perception of meaning that we draw on to make sense of something as ambiguous or unusual as a bar full of pigs.

● CONCEPT CHECKLIST

rhetoric	Aristotle	canons of rhetoric
logos	ethos	pathos
target audience	invention	arrangement
style	delivery	memory
typography	focal point	visual hierarchy
image continuum	schema theory	elements of design
principles of design		

● SUMMARY

- Media messages are rhetorical as they are meant to both inform and persuade.

- The canons of rhetoric can be applied to media messages for analysis

- The canons of rhetoric can be used as a structure, or framework, to message production.

- Identifying a target audience is imperative so that the message may be tailored to them.

- The canons of rhetoric are invention, arrangement, style, delivery, and memory.

- Invention provides a logical justification to a claim.

- Many messages are arranged with some form of an introduction, body, and conclusion.

- Visuals are arranged with a visual hierarchy, starting with a focal point.

- Visual message components are composed and arranged using the elements and principles of design.

- The style of a message can be categorized by its artful use of language and the approach to the visuals.

- Delivery refers to the method in which a message is conveyed or the manner in which a visual is rendered.

- The use of color and typography are aspects of style and delivery.

- We use aspects of schema theory, our powers of recall from our accumulated social knowledge, to interpret messages.

- A message can become more impactful by triggering memories.

● ACTIVITIES

1. Select several magazine or newspaper advertisements. Identify the target audience of the ad. Be as specific as you can with the demographic. What gender, age, income level, education level, marital status? How does the ad attract that audience?

2. Using the same ad as above, discuss how you would promote that same product or service to the opposite audience. How would you craft the message to this new audience?

3. Look through different magazines and newspapers for a variety of images that are rendered in different methods. Other than photographs, can you find images that are stylized using different techniques that may fit along the image continuum discussed in the chapter?

4. Analyze how type is used in print media through headlines and body copy. Then evaluate the use of type in the opening sequences of television programs or commercials.

5. Identify the visual hierarchy in a print piece. What is the focal point? Where does your eye travel next? Can you also identify the elements and principles of design that were used to compose the piece?

6. Conduct an analysis of a media text using Aristotle's five canons of rhetoric. Identify the audience, determine the claim and how the argument is justified through the rhetoric, discuss the arrangement and style, and how it is made memorable.

7. Using Aristotle's modes of persuasion, ethos, pathos, logos, can you identify the persuasive techniques used?

◉ REFERENCES

Books

The Non-Designer's Design Book
The Non-Designer's Type Book
by Robin Williams

Basic instruction books that are helpful with computers, desktop publishing, and design.

A Primer of Visual Literacy
by Dondis A. Dondis

Dondis provides a straightforward approach to visual communication in her book. The elements and principles of design are included, as well as Gestalt principles, and basic categories of style.

Articles

Linda Scott, "Images in Advertising: The Need for a Theory of Visual Rhetoric" *Journal of Consumer Research*, Vol. 21, 1994.

Definitely worth reading as the author applies the canons of rhetoric to advertising imagery and discusses various creative approaches used in advertising including the use of tropes.

Edward McQuarrie and David Glen Mick, "Visual Rhetoric in Advertising: Text-Interpretive, Experimental, and Reader-Response Analysis" *Journal of Consumer Research*, Vol. 26, 1999.

Another article that applies much of the concepts discussed in the chapter giving plenty of examples backed up by solid research.

◉ ENDNOTES

1. Beck and Sanderson,"Isocrates, Aristotle, and Diogenes," previously published in *Greece & Rome to 30 BC* <http://www.san.beck.org/EC22-Aristotle.html#4>.

2. Em Griffin, "The Rhetoric of Aristotle," *A First Look at Communication Theory*, 4th ed. (New York: McGraw-Hill, 2000, 275.

3. "Aristotle's Rhetoric," an online resource compiled by Lee Honeycutt, based on the translation of Aristotle's *Rhetoric* by W. Rhys Roberts. <http://www.public.iastate.edu/~honeyl/Rhetoric/index.html>.

4. Gideon O. Burton,"The Canons of Rhetoric," "Silva Rhetoricae," Brigham Young University, <http://rhetoric.byu.edu/canons/Canons.htm>

5. Griffin, "The Rhetoric of Aristotle," 280.

6. Griffin, "The Rhetoric of Aristotle," 276.

7. Lori Siebert and Lisa Ballard, *Making a Good Layout*, Northlight Books, Cincinatti, OH: 1992.

8. "Schema Theory of Learning" LingualLinks website, <http://www.sil.org/lingualinks/literacy/ImplementALiteracyProgram/SchemaTheoryOfLearning.htm> April 2008. Information derived from Anderson, Richard C., "The Notion of Schemata and the Educational Enterprise: General Discussion of the Conference," 1977.

9. Griffin, "The Rhetoric of Aristotle," 281.

10. Honeycutt, "Aristotle's Rhetoric"

Chapter 6

The Component of
Creative Language

Chapter Objectives

- Identify creative approaches used in media messages.
- Discuss the needs and desires that may be triggered by messages.
- Describe how messages attract the attention of the audience.
- Acquire the basic principles of photographic composition.

Key Media Literacy Concept #3:
Media messages are constructed using a creative language with its own rules.

Key Media Literacy Question #3:
What creative techniques are used to attract attention?

◉ CREATIVE APPROACHES

Competition for audience attention is intense due to the ever increasing means to connect to media and the prolific number of messages. Creators of media messages know that they have only seconds to grab the attention of the audience. To do so, they must use creative approaches to gain and hold the attention of the audience and then use a variety of appeals to both inform and influence.

This chapter, and this component of the Color Wheel Model of Media Communication, will explore the creative approaches and appeal strategies that work to gain our attention, as well as to entice us while creating a memorable work that both informs and entertains. If media messages use signs and symbols in a manner resembling a language, as previously discussed, then using artistic approaches to appeal to the audience is the creative language within the message. This artful crafting of a message also adds to its style. Therefore, this component of the Color Wheel Model extends the canon of style discussed in the previous chapter because we can identify the methods used to gain attention and place a creative spin on the message.

The creativity that goes into a message serves many purposes. First, a message is constructed to gain the attention of the audience. This must be accomplished in seconds or the audience will turn the channel, flip the page, or walk away. Second, a message must make an appeal to its audience by attracting them further into the message, luring them into the storyline, influencing thoughts and opinions, or creating desire for the product. Messages are then packaged so that the audience is being informed while they are entertained. Creative approaches aid in the amusement of the audience. Finally, creative approaches serve to differentiate one message from another, to aid in

of the multitude of messages, and by making an impact on the audience, a more memorable message is created.

A wide number of creative methods have proven to be very successful because they attract greater attention, are preferred by consumers, and are more memorable.[1] Many of the creative approaches and appeal strategies used in media messages play off our basic human instincts. Many of these are derived from theories of psychology, rhetoric, and consumer research. What follows is a sampling of common creative approaches and appeal strategies used in media messages.

● MASLOW'S HIERARCHY OF NEEDS

Abraham Maslow wrote *A Theory of Human Motivation* in 1943 defining a set of five basic human needs that were structured within a hierarchy.[2] Human beings are motivated to meet these needs satisfying the lower more fundamental needs before fulfilling those on higher levels of the hierarchy. This psychological theory of human motivation has been so widely accepted it is taught throughout higher education in a variety of disciplines and has been applied to a wide range of training initiatives for management, health care, and marketing. Recognizing that these are needs that humans strive to accomplish, media messages are created by tapping into these basic desires.

MASLOW'S HIERARCHY OF NEEDS

Maslow's five levels of human motivation can be used as a basis for appeal strategies in media messages.

PHYSIOLOGICAL NEEDS

The lowest and therefore most fundamental needs are those that the body must have satisfied to survive. These include water, air, food, and the appropriate temperature and amount of sleep. When deprived of these needs, the body begins to malfunction and behavior may change as it is a primal instinct to meet these needs.

SAFETY

Once the body's basic needs are met, the need for a secure environment is next. We seek shelter that protects us from weather, danger, predators, and other threats. Once free from fear or anxiety, a stability prevails that allows further movement up the hierarchy.

LOVE AND BELONGING

Once humans have the basic creature comforts, they seek love and affection through various relationships. Even within this area, there is a hierarchical structure to the relationships we seek. Our first relational level is with family on whom we rely for companionship and affection. We then develop wider relational groups connecting with friends and other social groups creating a network or community from which we gather a greater sense of belonging, developing bonds, and satisfying emotional needs.

ESTEEM

As we begin to develop a sense of belonging with others, we begin to seek recognition and respect from those relational groups. This acceptance and approval serves to build self-esteem within an individual creating a bi-level function to this level of the hierarchy—respect from others as well as self-respect.

SELF-ACTUALIZATION

Once all of the lower level needs are fulfilled, we reach a higher level of existence or development. At the top of the hierarchy is self-fulfillment where the realization of one's talents and potential is recognized. When our talents and ambitions are put to use to achieve individual goals, as well as for the greater good, a sense of appreciation for others and for life is attained.

● APPEAL STRATEGIES

While media packages can be constructed using creative approaches that provoke essential yearnings as described in Maslow's Hierarchy of Needs, there are many other tactics that can be used to appeal to an audience. Creative approaches to message production may be achieved through a variety of techniques and serve to present something familiar in an original way. These imaginative messages present information in an entertaining manner and are highly used in advertising.

Strategies like humor and sexual appeal are often the most predominant techniques used in media to entice an audience. Emotional appeals have a profound effect as they leave both a mental and emotional impression. Many scholars have studied the effects of rhetorical approaches, particularly in advertising, and have found them to be very effective.[3] Because they are more original, audiences find these approaches more stimulating, even pleasurable.[4] Therefore, they have a greater impact on the audience, making them more memorable.[5]

Above all, a message must be tailored to the cognitive abilities of the audience as understanding the ability of the public to interpret the message will dictate the means in which it is created as a message that is too creative or too abstract may be ineffective.

Many scholars and advertising practitioners have compiled lists of effective appeal strategies.[6] What follows is a collection of some of the most recognizable strategies used within media messages.

HUMOR

As stated earlier, humor is a common approach used in advertising messages, television programs, films, and a variety of other media packages. Super Bowl ads thrive on this strategy where amusing anecdotes, comic situations, and jokes abound. Situation comedies exaggerate family situations, late-night comedy shows capitalize on events of the day, and even news broadcasts integrate a lighthearted or humorous story in an effort to balance the array of issues and concerns that were reported on.

EMOTIONAL APPEALS

Aristotle understood the power of emotion as he included pathos, or the emotional appeal, in the artistic proofs he outlined to construct a persuasive argument. Emotional appeals are a very common approach and can be as varied as the range of human emotion.

Media messages using this approach have an enormous impact as they can effectively influence an audience on both a cognitive, or mental, level as well as on an emotional level. A sentimental or tender storyline may bring a tear to our eye, or we may feel nostalgic when a product reminiscent of something from our past is promoted in an ad, or feel great joy when watching a favorite team win a championship.

However, emotional appeals do not have to be positive to be effective. Fear is a powerful emotion and an equally effective approach. Home security and insurance companies often use fear as an effective means to promote their services particularly with images of natural disasters or home invasions.

SEX APPEAL

We have all heard it; "sex sells." Sexual appeals are used to sell everything from clothing to body lotions, perfumes, lingerie, cars, tools, auto parts, food products, and more. The attempt to create allure, even tempt or seduce an audience, runs the gamut from subtle to sultry. However, care must be taken that the state of dress, or undress, the provocative poses and subject matter, either actual or implied, do not offend the audience.

Over the years, Victoria Secrets ad campaigns for bras, lingerie and perfume have received much attention, and criticism. The marketing images used by Abercrombie and Fitch, black-and-white images of young males and females with a tendency to show more flesh than clothing, has also been the subject of both admiration and ridicule.

AFFILIATION, PROMINENCE, ACHIEVEMENT

While Maslow's hierarchy identifies our need for esteem, this appeal elevates this need as it is nice to have gained respect but better to be revered. This level of accomplishment may be attained by achieving a level of prominence in our jobs or in our community, and by associating with others who have done the same. This strategy is often used to promote luxury items such as cars, jewelry, and designer clothing.

ATTRACTING ATTENTION

Drawing attention to oneself to be noticed is a primal desire. Clothing and cosmetic companies use this strategy extensively, drawing attention to their products but also suggesting that by using those products the consumer will become the "object of fascination." Promos for news programs often use this approach to create awareness for stories in their upcoming broadcast.

AESTHETIC SENSATIONS

We are drawn to beauty. Beautiful imagery will attract us. Some magazines are filled with beautiful photography, people, homes, cars, or food. Glamour shots of these subjects serve to pleasure our sense of beauty but also create a desire in us to have the same. This is a primary approach in advertising for cosmetics and beauty products, but is also used by furniture stores, home centers, and car accessories. Television programming and even whole networks have been designed to help us beautify our homes and yards.

NEED TO NURTURE OR TO BE NURTURED

This appeal strategy extends Maslow's need to love and belonging as there is both a need to take care of others and also to be cared for. We are drawn to images of innocent children and animals as well as the pleas to come to their aid. As much as we are willing to care for others, we also want to have someone guide and protect us as well.

Various personal care products promise to care for us body and soul, as do health care and pharmaceutical companies. Investment companies will lead us to a secure retirement, while leaving something for our families, and even airlines market personal service and consideration for the comfort and convenience of their travelers.

ESCAPE

Our hectic lives often leave us scrambling for any means to escape the frenzied routine. Freedom may be sought through travel or a simple cup of coffee overlooking a quiet vista. The idea is to elude the daily regimen and to seek rest or adventure, whether that be by a vacation, leisurely drive away from the chaos, or a backyard bonfire with family.

HEALTH

The media is full of messages about the unhealthy lifestyle we are leading, the rise in various health concerns, and the many ways to improve our well-being. To help with our eating habits, we can subscribe to meal services for ourselves, and even our pets. Service companies will scan our homes for hidden health concerns, like radon, due to our heavily insulated homes.

PLEASURE

This creative approach appeals to the child in us all, as the messages tell us that it is acceptable to take pleasure in something for the pure enjoyment of it. We read a book for the contentment it brings us, or enticed to amusement parks or recreation facilities for the sheer fun of it.

This is a predominant theme for tobacco advertising. As the regulations state they cannot advertise on television, are limited to magazines with an audience that is predominately over 18, and must include a warning from the Surgeon General on their packaging.[7] Most importantly they have even been discouraged from including informational claims about their product's content. Without the ability to advertise the product, it has left little for the industry to promote except pleasure.[8]

ENVIRONMENTAL CONCERNS

The threat of global warming has led to a surge of messages appealing for the health of our planet and the means by which we as individuals can adapt our lifestyles, curb consumption of non-sustainable goods, and adapt to alternative energy resources in the effort to "go green."

CONVENIENCE

With our increasingly busy lives we are always looking for ways to make life easier, to achieve a goal faster, and to do so with as little effort as possible. We can buy pills for weight loss without the need to diet and pre-packaged food that we must only heat in a microwave to serve.

CELEBRITY

More and more celebrities including actors, athletes, and musicians are lending their talents and persona to sell a variety of products or act as spokespersons for organizations and their interests. The recognition of these well known people adds credibility to the cause or product.

POP CULTURE

An element from another form of popular media like a gesture, a distinctive feature from a character, or the fashion they are known for, can add a unique element to a message. A James Bond-like character can add a different influence than a typical male model.

FALLACIES

There are many media messages that focus on falsehoods or illusions to create unrealistic expectations, situations, or imagery. We have all seen advertising imagery like that at right, with an expectation that the product will magically clear one's complexion yet the two images are identical and obviously manipulated. Likewise, remedies for the common cold that promise instantaneous

cures are promoting a fallacy. Though we know that this doesn't happen in real life, these ads are selling hope as much as the product.

FANTASY

Similar to fallacy there is an element of unrealistic expectations in this approach that utilizes fantasy, yet this imaginative technique amplifies creativity with manufactured elements of make-believe. Plenty of films, commercials, television shows, and ads use this extraordinary or magical approach.

THE UNEXPECTED

Graphic designers and other creators of media messages are supposed to "think out of the box." This term signifies the need for the designer to use a creative approach that may be a bit out of the ordinary, a little risky, or unconventional. Doing so enables these messages to be original and stimulating, to have greater impact, and be more memorable. The use of unusual imagery prevails in advertising and print media.

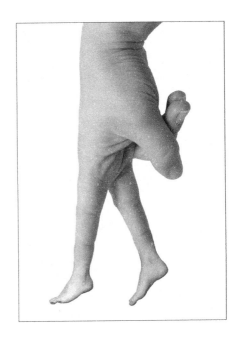

Various studies have proven that unusual images have a greater effect on audiences,[9] in fact, the more deviant the device the greater the impact.[10] Images that are unexpected also attract greater attention and are more memorable.[11]

In film and television unexpected plot twists and surprise endings create impact.

Advertising images that use nostalgia as an emotional appeal are effective at cutting through ad clutter as well as triggering memories.

NOSTALGIA

As an appeal strategy in advertising nostalgia is an emotional approach that draws on sentimental past associations and our fondness for days gone by.

The piece seen here uses a style reminiscent of another era and is a paradoy of the recruitment poster created by James Montgomery Flagg in 1917.[12] Uncle Sam has since become a personification of the United States governement.

These visual parodies not only recycle a visual trend but also trigger memories, as discussed in the previous chapter, which can create a memorable piece and help it cut through the clutter.

◉ OGILVY'S ADVERTISING TACTICS

It is worth reviewing successful advertising tactics since advertisements are predominant media messages.

The late David Ogilvy, was a brilliant advertising executive with a number of successful high-profile ad campaigns.[13] He outlined several distinctive tactics in his book, *Ogilvy on Advertising*. These key concepts are still used successfully today.[14]

DEMONSTRATIONS

Demonstrating the product in use is a very effective tactic that allows an audience to see what a product does while displaying the product's attributes and effectiveness. This is the tactic that infomercials employ to not only exhibit their products but to demonstrate what the product is capable of doing.

TESTIMONIALS

Testimonials are product endorsements given by actual users, celebrities, or actors. This tactic is used extensively by Proactiv Solution, an acne treatment system, that features clips of actual users of the product including prominent celebrity users.

TALKING HEADS

This tactic is often used to promote services when there is no product to demonstrate such as legal or financial services. Talking heads are essentially "pitchmen extolling the virtues of a product." [15]

CHARACTERS

Characters are personalities played by actors or even cartoon characters used to pitch a product. They become the "recognizable face" of the product like Flo for Progressive insurance, the Pillsbury doughboy, the Aflac duck, the Geico gecko, or the many cartoon characters used to sell cereal from the Fruit Loops toucan to Frosted Flakes' Tony the Tiger.

SLICE OF LIFE

This ad tactic uses seemingly everyday people going about their regular lives when they are presented with a significant situation that many of us can relate to, and may be seeking a resolution for. In these "playlets" one person espouses the value of a product. For instance, at the bus stop a passenger tells a man waiting in line that his bank offers free checking while in another someone spills a cup of coffee and their friend tells them that her brand of paper towels absorbs more and lasts longer. This sharing of information is an approach that is easy to relate to.

PROBLEM-SOLUTION

Many products are purchased because they solve a problem for the user. Cold remedies rid us of annoying cold symptoms, and laundry detergents clean the most stubborn stains.

REASON WHY

This tactic is as basic as gets—tell the audience why they need to buy the product using a logical reason. This technique is used quite often in the service industry such as when your heating or air conditioning quits during an extreme weather situation, on a weekend, in the middle of the morning, but are reminded of the local professional with 24-hour service.

NEWS

This category serves to highlight news to report about a product. This includes new or improved products as well as products that have become known for uses other than its initial, intended use. Pinterest is full of life-hacks of common products with uncommon uses. For instance Vaseline petroleum jelly can silence a squeaky door and is good for a quick shoe shine. Basic white Colgate toothpaste gets scuff marks off shoes and floors. [16]

Probably the best known product with multiple uses is baking soda which, of course, is primarily used in baking. Ad campaigns have promoted its use as a refrigerator freshener, but did you know it can also be used as an antacid, a toothpaste, to remove badly burned on food from pans, or clean the coffee maker? The Arm and Hammer Company has actually embraced the extended use of its product devoting a whole section of their website to some of these alternatives. [17]

● STYLISTIC DEVICES

Stylistic or rhetorical devices are creative approaches derived from language such as metaphors, simile, puns, and irony. These figures of speech, also known as tropes, add interest by providing a twist on the familiar and can be used traditionally within the text of a message or in a visual manner through the imagery.

The use of rhetorical figures is a creative approach that is recognized in design publications and taught in classrooms, although graphic designers tend to lump several of these devices under the umbrella of "metaphor," [18] in particular, the first three tropes listed here metaphor, simile, and analogy.

Several studies have analyzed the use of rhetorical strategies in advertising and indicated that, although abstract, they are effective. Data indicated that these ads performed better through both recall and persuasive means. [19]

METAPHOR

Aristotle specifically mentioned the use of metaphor as an effective use of style. A metaphor uses an unrelated object to describe another and are among the most common stylistic devices used in media messages. In visual media images are used to represent concepts as was discussed earlier in semiotics where the image of the dove was said to be a recognizable symbol for peace. Here the Rolls-Royce can be used to represent wealth.

A metaphor uses an unrelated object to describe another, in this case the car represents wealth.

SIMILE

A simile compares two objects that share an attribute or feature. In a magazine ad for Nexium a slice of pizza morphs into a wood saw. The saw represents the pain incurred by many who suffer from acid reflux where stomach acid backs up into the esophagus causing inflammation and abrasions in the esophagus. The symbolism is that the acidic and spicy aspect of the pizza is like a saw cutting through the esophageal wall.

ANALOGY

Visual analogies compare two unrelated objects on the basis of a similar feature. A coiled up garden hose and a coiled snake are similar in appearance.

PERSONIFICATION

Personification is the application of human characteristics to a non-human entity. This is often done in television commercials, films, and children's book illustrations where animals have the ability to talk and to reason.

HYPERBOLE

Hyperbole is the use of extreme exaggeration to make a point. Claims can be unrealistically distorted without offering any evidence to back them up, and images can make something look larger or distorted.

IRONY

Irony uses language or imagery that signifies a meaning opposite of the what is expected. For example, an image of an SUV with a bumper sticker that says "Save the planet" is ironic.

PUNS

A pun is a humorous play on words but in the visual media messages must use visual elements that create the effect. In this example there is an image of a "green house." Not only do we understand "green" to be a color, but also a term to describe the concept of environmental responsibility. This house is not only green in color but is made of grass.

EPANAPHORA

Epanaphora uses repetition for emphasis. A repetitive message can create a sense of recognition, familiarity, and expectation in an audience while a recurring phrase in the text serves to instill a message into the mind of the consumer. Imagery that uses this approach often takes repetition to an extreme by repeating elements not just a few times but in mass for a dramatic effect.

SYNECDOCHE

The trope of synecdoche is used to represent a concept by using only a part of the object; in other words, the part represents the whole. Visually this is done using a severely cropped image, cropped to the point one almost has to guess what the object is. In this example, we only see a portion of the athletic shoe.

● APPROACHES CAN BE COMBINED

It is important to note that although the creative strategies that have been summarized here are among the most common, there are others. It is also essential to understand that these creative approaches can be combined. For instance, the example below uses several different creative approaches to attract and keep our attention.

The image is definitely unusual; in fact, the idea of the dog pulling his master in this manner is overly exaggerated. The ability of such a small dog being capable of pulling his master is ironic and even humorous. So this image uses four different approaches: something unexpected, hyperbole, irony, and humor.

Although highly effective in advertising, these strategies can be used effectively by any form of media to attract attention of the audience, entertain while informing, and be more memorable.

⦿ CASE IN POINT

IDENTIFYING CREATIVE APPROACHES

As evidenced by the previous examples there are many ways to attract the attention of the audience and draw them into a piece. By taking a more comprehensive look at the example ad for Trojan brand condoms, we can deconstruct it to identify the strategies used and evaluate their ability to capture the audience and to create meaning.

Use of the Trojan® Warrior Head Logo® and EVOLVE.™ trademarks, and EVOLVE print ad for TROJAN® brand Condoms is with the express written permission of Church & Dwight Co., Inc, Princeton, New Jersey. TROJAN, EVOLVE, and the Warrior Head logo are trademarks of Church & Dwight Virginia Co., Inc. © Church & Dwight Virginia Co., Inc. 2007.

Identifying the creative approaches

There are several creative approaches used to grab the attention of the audience within this piece, and most are associated with the use of the imagery of the pigs.

The Unexpected

The use of pigs as the primary clientele in the bar creates an unusual image, which immediately attracts the audience's attention,

Personification

The beer drinking, electronic device using pigs provide human characteristics to a non-human entity–the embodiment of the classic application of personification.

Humor

The approach of the personified pigs is also initially humorous.

Epanaphora

The repetitiveness of the pigs, particularly as the dominate occupants of the bar, is an example of epanaphora. Pigs outnumber humans in this image by almost 2:1. The repetition of the pigs serves to drive the point home.

Metaphor

The metaphorical pigs are characters representing the inconsiderate male in this little drama, which has greater implications, as sex appeal plays a role in the quest for love and belonging and finding the "right one."

One could even extend the creative approaches to include Health and Love and Belonging. All of these creative approaches deviate from the expected affording the piece greater impact.

Don't forget to apply what you already know

You've probably noticed that this analysis has applied information from several of the previous components of the Color Wheel Model. As discussed in chapter 3, the components of the Color Wheel have concepts that overlap each other

When performing an analysis, it is always best to go back to the beginning, the list of basic building blocks–the denotative elements and connotative meaning– as the inventory that we can apply our concepts to.

In this case, the pigs and humans are the primary denotative elements that create the metaphor behind the connotative meaning for men to evolve by choosing to be a responsible male and use a condom.

Analyzing the creative strategies used in media messages is significant to becoming media literate. However, since most of our media is visual, it is imperative to recognize the techniques behind the imagery. In the last chapter, the Component of Structure detailed several methods in which to create and deliver images. We learned that there are different elements employed to design imagery, and different means in which to deliver them. Imagery falls on a continuum from the most realistic through various levels of abstraction. Photography begins that continuum as the most realistic. Learning to identify the different approaches to photographic style aids in both analysis and developing an appreciation for the skill involved.

● PHOTOGRAPHIC STYLE

Photography is subjective by nature, as it is dependent on what one chooses to put in the viewfinder. In a three-dimensional world, one must choose which view to shoot, and to also choose what to omit. Much of this is quite typical. Who hasn't been in a situation where in trying to get a picture of a famous landmark a group of tourists wanders into the frame? Patiently the photographer waits as the group moves away to take the shot clear of the complete strangers. By waiting for the right opportunity, the photographer has made a strategic choice about what to photograph—and what not to. Now let's extend this example a bit more. If the photographer had arrived on the scene to find construction scaffolding on part of the landmark, and chose to crop out that section to create a more pleasing photograph, then again a choice was made about what to include as well as what to exclude. Is choosing to omit this extraneous information only telling part of the story? While the subjectivity and omissions of the photographer are considerations in analysis, there is much information to be gained in determining how a photograph was taken, and why it is significant to the message.

Photographic principles including the basic types of camera shots along with the various camera angles and viewpoints, composition, lighting, and focus have an impact on creating impactful imagery. Exposure to basic photographic skills enables one to not only analyze and evaluate imagery in media messages, but to produce better images as well. Many amateur photographers take snapshots with simple cameras, yet learning these principles, can elevate the typical snapshot to a much higher level. Therefore, this section can be used as both a lesson in analysis, as well as a summary of basic techniques to employ when producing imagery.

BASIC PHOTOGRAPHIC SHOTS

The fundamental shots are based on the distance between the camera and the subject. In a long shot, the subject is a distance from the photographer and is often used to establish the scene or environment that the subject is in, or to take a shot without disturbing the subject often resulting in a more natural subject. Due to the wide expanse it is also called a wide or full shot.

A medium shot is, as it sounds, a photograph taken at a medium distance to the subject. This is the distance typical for many amateur photographers, as they tend to take most of their images at this "safe" distance, not too close and too far away from their subjects.

A close-up moves in closer and is used to place the focus entirely on the subject, often excluding extraneous information that might distract from the subject.

An extreme close-up is used to show intense detail of a subject.

Varying viewpoints—
The images of the
U.S. Capitol seen here are
examples of a long shot,
medium shot, and close-up.

CAMERA ANGLE

Once the photographer determines how close to get to a subject, he or she must decide what angle to take the shot from. Most amateur photographers typically choose the easiest camera angle– directly from the front at eye level–but a change in angle and perspective can create a more dramatic shot. Change position to the side, behind, above or below for additional points of view.

These images of the Eiffel Tower illustrate the varying shots that can be achieved when taking in the subject from the front, from the side, and even from below.

Low Level Shots

Using a low angle and shooting up at a subject can make the subject appear more imposing or majestic. Ground level shots can offer an unusual perspective of a subject.

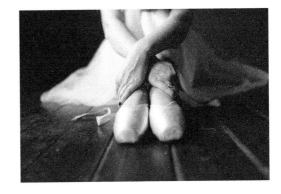

Babies and pets should be photographed at their eye level, rather than at the photographer's eye level. Choosing the lower angle captures the subject in a far more natural position than looking up into the camera extending their necks unnaturally, and is also more intimate.

Overhead Shots

Sometimes the best vantage point is to rise above the subject, again, offering a different perspective such as the ballerina at right. Crowds are best shot from above, since to shoot among the crowd would result in nothing but the heads and shoulders of those directly in front of the camera lens.

COMPOSITION

As stated, the view through the camera lens is subjective. The photographer chooses what to focus on and what to omit. Positioning the lens is essentially an act of composition, or artfully arranging the subject within the viewfinder.

Cropping

Omitting background information allows the image to enhance one area giving it a specific focus., However, we must not crop out information that would provide context. While it is not normal to advocate cropping a subject's head off, in this case the focus is not the model, but her hand and the jewelry.

Balance

Typically a subject is centered in the viewfinder creating symmetrical balance, but an asymmetrical subject may be more dramatic. Compositionally, this technique is known as the rule of thirds and there are a number of reasons to use it.

THE RULE OF THIRDS

One of the most effective ways to create asymmetrical balance, and a much more dramatic shot, is to use a principle called the rule of thirds. The foolproof method is achieved by dividing the viewfinder into thirds, both horizontally and vertically, and placing the subject on one of the intersecting points, as in the diagram at below left.

The landscape below places the lone tree on the same intersecting grids.

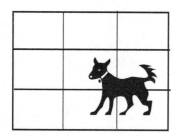 

Allowing for Movement

Besides being more dramatic, the rule of thirds allows space for a moving subject to move into as with the image of the knight on the charging horse.

Space to Look Into

The rule of thirds can be used for portraiture as well. Allow space for your subject to gaze into rather than cutting off the frame in front of their face.

LEADING LINES

Using leading lines or strong diagonals, through the frame creates a means to lead the eye through the image called continuation. The image on this page of the bridge and sailboat, use both strong diagonals and the rule of thirds.

FRAME WITHIN A FRAME

Framing a subject using a naturally occurring element is a compositional technique that draws the eye in to the subject while creating depth and giving the subject context.

The image at left, uses the arches of the colonnade to frame the ruins of the abbey behind it.

FOCUS

Cameras with manual controls allow for a variety of focal settings. Adjusting these setting can produce a variety of effects. Filters that are placed on the lens can also alter the appearance of an image.

Hard and Soft Focus

Normally we want an image to be clear and sharp, also known as hard focus, but the mood of an image can change as quickly as the focal settings. An image with a soft focus can create a subtle effect that can give it a quiet, romantic, or dreamy quality as in the image seen at right.

Depth of Field

Normally when focusing on a subject closer to the camera, the background objects will appear blurry or out of focus, and conversely when centering on an object further away the foreground will be out of focus. The image of the abbey above, is completely in focus, both in the foreground as well as the background. The image is said to have a long focal length and can be accomplished with a little math and the right lenses.

LIGHTING

There are a variety of ways to light a subject through the use of a camera-mounted flash, studio lighting, or natural lighting.

Flash Photography

The use of a flash is important when there is not enough ambient light to illuminate your subject. Care should be taken with artificial lighting, as many amateur photographers tend to overexpose their subject by getting too close with a flash as in the first example below. Moving back from the subject allows for a correctly exposed image.

At times the camera may register enough ambient light but the subject may be in the shade. This is when the photographer must use a fill flash by overriding an automatic setting, forcing the flash to fire.

Studio Lighting

Flash units are usually bounced into special umbrellas softening the effect of the flash, which can create dramatic results.

Shots that focus on the subject using artful positioning and lighting are often called hero shots and are meant to glamorize an individual, product, building, or corporate brand.

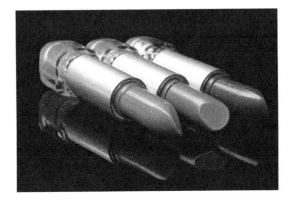

NATURAL LIGHTING

Much thought needs to be taken when capturing a subject in daylight. The harsh light of the midday sun in the example at right creates harsh shadows that produce an eerie effect by hollowing the eyes of this young girl.

The softer light of morning, a few hours after sunrise, or evening hours before sunset are better for portrait photography.

Day vs. Night

If one is patient enough to explore natural lighting during the course of the day, and into the night, dramatic results are often the result as seen here with the images of the Eiffel Tower. The most magical time of day to capture the dramatic natural light is the Golden Hour just before sunrise or sunset, from the soft glow of morning to the dramatic blue of twilight.

Backlighting

When the light source originates behind the subject, the effect can be quite dramatic. Care must be taken when backlighting a subject, as it is necessary to use the subject to completely block the light source so as not to create a lens flare. When done well, the subject will be illuminated from behind creating a slight silhouette effect.

PHOTO MANIPULATION

This examination of photography has focused on the different techniques used to compose a shot through the viewfinder, however it started by stating that photography is the most realistic form of imagery. While primarily true, the technology that exists today can easily alter reality. With digital imaging and computer software, like Adobe Photoshop, which is designed to edit photographs, the old adage "seeing is believing" should now be questioned.

Perfecting the Imperfect

With current digital hardware and software flawed images can be perfected. Freeing images from defects is used widely in commercial applications such as advertising.

The images of the waterfront in Buffalo, New York, were taken by the author while designing a project for a nonprofit organization. The results of this traditional film image was disappointing because it was crooked, blurry, and cropped the bottom of the sailboat. It was necessary to alter the image. The results, at right, show an image in focus, with a re-created sky and water, and a completed boat.

This same concept of perfecting flaws is used widely in the fashion and advertising industries, where reflections in car windows are eliminated, creases in clothing smoothed over, and models are altered. Our expectations of perfection have been changed as a result.

Creating Fantasy

While manipulation can perfect flaws, it can also create a different reality. Images can be morphed together to create fantastic combinations, like the example here, the unusual image on page 115, or the metaphorical pigs in a bar in the Trojan ad analyzed through out the book. Impossible situations or characters can be created, ordinary objects can be combined creating an incongruous image, and the norm can be altered.

Artistic Approaches

Images can be altered for the sake of creating a form of art. Again images can be manipulated, morphed together, and filters within the software can create a variety of effects.

The Ethics of Manipulation

Unlike the tangible proof of an unaltered film negative, a digital image exists only within the pixels of a computer until printed out. The ease of alteration has even caused the courts, and law enforcement agencies, to adapt new methods of evidence handling and storage.

The alteration of imagery is not permissible in photojournalism. The primary responsibility of any journalist, reporter, or photojournalist is to "seek the truth and report it." The ability, and use, of digital manipulation has called into question the ethics of such practice.

Editorial images have been altered, even before digital capabilities by staging or re-creating events, through cropping, and with photo illustrations. This still occurs in the industry today, but the ease of altering reality has been carried out by several magazines and newspapers. Two obvious and well-known examples of this manipulation occurred when *National Geographic* moved the pyramids of Egypt closer together to fit the narrow format of their cover, and *Time* altered the image of O. J. Simpson's mug shot for the cover of their magazine.

These applications are frowned upon, yet media applications are a paradox–we expect the truth, yet are intrigued by originality and perfection.

⊙ CONCEPT CHECKLIST

Maslow's Hierarchy of Needs	creative approaches
appeal strategies	stylistic devices (or tropes)
metaphor	emotional appeal
camera shots	camera angle
compositional techniques	rule of thirds
leading lines	lighting techniques
digital manipulation	

⊙ SUMMARY

- Maslow's Hierarchy of Needs identifies five levels of human motivation that can be used as a basis for creative approaches in media messages.

- Creative approaches provide the twist in the communication of media messages.

- These creative approaches and appeal strategies are successful because they are preferred by consumers and are more memorable.

- There are a substantial number of methods of creative approaches used in the media today but humor, sex, and the emotional appeal are among the most widely used.

- Tactics used in media messages are effective in promoting a product.

- Stylistic devices, or tropes, are creative approaches that are borrowed from language.

- Composition, lighting, and subject matter often differentiates between a snapshot and the art of photography

- There are a variety of compositional approaches to photography including the choices in the various shots, camera angles, and framing, including the use of techniques such as the rule of thirds, and leading lines.

- Images can be manipulated using digital software and hardware.

- There are ethical concerns involved in digitally manipulating an image.

● ACTIVITIES

1. Gather a variety of magazines and review the ads. Identify the creative approaches that were used. How many different strategies can you find? Does any one approach dominate? Does it depend on the source or target audience? Are there any visual tropes? Is there evidence of digital manipulation?

2. Select an ad using sex appeal. Interview men and women of different ages to determine if they find it appealing. What are some of the reactions? Do they differ by gender? by age? Discuss it in a group setting to hear a variety of perspectives.

3. How many characters, like Tony the Tiger, can you list that promote products or services?

4. Watch an infomercial. How many different tactics do they use?

5. Analyze a tobacco ad. How do they promote the product?

6. Go online and review spoof ads for various products. *Adbusters* is well known for their creative spoof ads for products in the fashion, tobacco, alcohol, and food industries.

7. Search the Internet for lifehacks for regular everyday products like baking soda. Any useful tip? What seems the most far-fetched?

8. Can you assess the photographic style and compositional techniques that are used in media imagery?

● RESOURCES

Books

David Ogilvy, *Ogilvy on Advertising,* John Wiley and Sons, Toronto and Pan Books, London (1983).

The late principle of Ogilvy & Mather wrote several books on the subject of advertising. This one provides a straight forward approach to the subject.

Websites

The most magical time of day to capture landscapes and dramatic natural light is the Golden Hour just before sunrise or sunset. Though called the Golden Hour for the intensity of color, the peak time available for these shots is actually much shorter. There are several websites and apps that offer tutorials and calculators that identify the exact range and peak for the time in your specific location. This is one of them: BlueHourSite **https://www.bluehoursite.com/**

Articles

Scott, Linda."Images in Advertising: The Need for a Theory of Visual Rhetoric." *Journal of Consumer Research*, 21 (1994).

McQuarrie, E. and Mick, D. "Visual Rhetoric in Advertising: Text-Interpretive, Experimental, and Reader-Response Analysis." *Journal of Consumer Research*, 26 (1999).

McQuarrie, E. and Mick, D. "Figures of Rhetoric in Advertising Language." *Journal of Consumer Research*, 22, (1996): 424–438.

Phillips, B. "Thinking Into It: Consumer Interpretation of Complex Advertising Images." *Journal of Advertising*, 26 (1997): 77–87.

⊙ ENDNOTES

1. G. Tom and A. Eves "The Use of Rhetorical Devices in Advertising." *Journal of Advertising Research*, (Aug/Sep) (1999): 39–43.

2. A. Maslow, "A Theory of Human Motivation," *Psychological Review*, 50, (1943), 370–396.

3. Several scholars have conducted research regarding the effectiveness of creative approaches, particularly rhetorical devices in advertising including articles by G. Tom and A. Eves (1999), L. Scott (1994), E. McQuarrie and D. Mick (1999), and B. Phillips (1997). See Resources.

4. Edward McQuarrie and David Glen Mick, "Visual Rhetoric in Advertising: Text-Interpretive, Experimental, and Reader-Response Analysis" *Journal of Consumer Research*, Vol. 26, 1999.

5. Tom and Eves, "The Use of Rhetorical Devices in Advertising."

6. The list of creative approaches was compiled from a variety of sources including Jib Fowels's "Advertising's Fifteen Basic Appeals" The piece was an excerpt from *Common Culture: Reading and Writing About American Popular Culture*, edited by Michael Petracca and Madeleine Sorapure. Upper Saddle River, NJ: Prentice Hall, 1998 and found online at <http://www.cyberpat.com/shirlsite/education/essay2/jfowles.html>. David Ogilvy also outlined several strategies in his book, *Ogilvy on Advertising.*

7. "Federal Regulation of Tobacco" American Heart Association, July 1, 2008 <http://www.americanheart.org/presenter.jhtml?identifier=11223>

8. John E. Calfee, "The Ghost of Cigarette Advertising Past," *Regulation*, 10, no. 02 (1986); reprinted in 20, no. 3 (1997).

9. Information compiled from a variety of sources including: Paul Messaris, *Visual Persuasion: The Role of Images in Advertising.* Thousand Oaks, CA: Sage Publications (1997), as well as previously cited articles by McQuarrie and Mick, 1996, and Tom and Eves, 1999.

10. E. McQuarrie and D. Mick, "Figures of Rhetoric in Advertising Language." *Journal of Consumer Research*, 22, (1996): 424–438.

11. Scott, Linda, "Images in Advertising: The Need for a Theory of Visual Rhetoric." *Journal of Consumer Research*, 21 (1994).

12. Knauer, Kelly. "I Want You: The Story Behind the Iconic Recruitment Poster." Time Books, 2017. <https://time.com/4725856/uncle-sam-poster-history/>

13. "David Ogilvy Remembered," History Ogilvy & Mather <http://www.ogilvy.com/history/>

14. David Ogilvy, *Ogilvy on Advertising,* Toronto, Canada: John Wiley and Sons, 1983.

15. David Ogilvy, *Ogilvy on Advertising.*

16. The uses for other products listed here are the author's own alternative uses for these products. Many more can be found online; Google uses for additional products.

17. "Baking Soda Products," Arm and Hammer website <https://www.armandhammer.com/en/baking-soda/baking-soda-products> June 2020. Other creative approaches have been compiled from a variety of sources as well as the author's own observation.

18. Landa, R. (1998). *Thinking Creatively: New Ways to Unlock Your Imagination*, Cincinnati, OH:Northlight Books.

19. Tom and Eves, "The Use of Rhetorical Devices in Advertising." (1999).

Chapter 7

The Component of
Media Operations

Chapter Objectives

- Identify the different forms of mass media.
- Examine the developmental characteristics of each medium.
- Discuss the trends in the media industry.
- Evaluate the influence the media has on our society.
- Understand the scope of the media business.
- Produce a media message.

Key Media Literacy Concept #4:
Media messages are constructed to gain profit and/or power and have embedded values and points of view.

Key Media Literacy Question #4:
What lifestyles, values, and points of view are represented in, or omitted from, this message?

• •

◉ THE POWER OF THE MEDIA

After a message has been carefully crafted using signs and symbols to create denotative and connotative meaning and has been structured to attract a target audience with its creative approach, it must be made available to the public through media. Any comprehensive analysis of media messages must then examine the means in which these messages are distributed. This component of the Color Wheel Model will identify the forms of media, examine their individual characteristics, and explain the various trends of the media business.

This book opened with a discussion of the prevalence of the media, our incomparable access and rampant consumption. Yet because this extensive use is often seen as merely a form of entertainment or information, we think nothing of the stealth in which we are impacted by the media messages. A greater concern is the lack of understanding regarding how the media is structured and the power behind it.

This power is twofold—the psychological power over the audience and power by its sheer dominance. The effects of the media have been studied extensively resulting in a vast number of papers, books, and even entire classes devoted exclusively to this subject. Therefore a thorough examination here would be impossible. A brief appraisal of some of the theories will be offered to gain a better understanding of the complexities and influences of media messages.

When asked, people often identify the media's role in society as that of a source of information and entertainment, and sometimes as an educational source. Media research has identified a number of theories that illustrate how we use media for a variety of purposes, as well as the psychological influence it has upon us.

● MEDIA THEORIES

USES AND GRATIFICATIONS THEORY

In an earlier chapter, the changing landscape of media consumption was discussed as well as the effects of that media has on us.

The Uses and Gratifications model, created in 1974, by Jay G. Blumler and Elihu Katz asserts that people use media to fulfill various needs.[1] Much like Maslow discussed a hierarchy of needs based on human motivation, the uses and gratification model outlines five different areas of motivation for using media: escape, social interaction, identity creation, information/education, and entertainment.

Escape is again similar to Maslow's description where we seek distractions or relief from our existence here using media as an escapist form of entertainment. There are many different forms of media that one can use to escape, whether it is to pop into a movie theater for an hour or two, snuggle in with a book, or spend the night on the couch watching the latest marathon of a favorite show.

*Media fulfills
a need and we
need different
forms of media
for different
reasons at
different times.*

The element of social interaction states that we develop relationships with various media characters. We may only watch a particular newscast because we have come to know and feel comfortable and trusting of the anchor of that newscast. Often fans of a particular character in a book or television show know minute details about that character. There are such devout fans of the *Star Wars* films and *Star Trek* series that they attend conventions dressed as various characters from these entertainment venues. Fans of this nature are usually quite protective of the characters, or media professionals, that they have come to be connected to seeking them out in other venues, defending them in adversity, and grieving at their loss.

We can also develop our own sense of identity through various forms of media. Identity creation is the ability to refine our individual identities based on elements observed in media texts that appeal to us. Magazines and newspapers often display the latest fashions and the current trends in home decor for us to emulate. Books, films, and television create characters and character traits to imitate, which might include anything from a manner of dress or hairstyle, to an uttered phrase, gesture, or behavior.

The last two areas of the uses and gratification model, information/education and entertainment, are fairly self-explanatory; media is used as a tool to gain information, including that which will provide instruction and increased knowledge and as a means of enjoyment.

Essentially uses and gratification posits that media is used for a variety of reasons, and that we choose to use those that satisfy and fulfill our needs at any given time.

DEPENDENCY THEORY

In 1976, Sandra Ball-Rokeach and Melvin DeFleur proposed this theory, which combines aspects of uses and gratifications research with those of other media effects research.[2] This model also states that we choose forms of media that meet our needs, but extends the idea of preference to that of dependency, because today we are more dependent on media for both our information and entertainment.

We are less physically active, preferring the entertainment of our collections of streaming services, social media, and video games to more active pastimes. However, by preferring these more solitary pursuits, we have also become less involved in our communities. Few attend town board or school board meetings, become active in community organizations, or have first-hand knowledge of community issues. We rely on the media as our primary source to not only inform us, but decipher the information for us. As with uses and gratifications theory, if we like and agree with the point of view of a particular newscast or publication, we will return to that as a primary source of entertainment or news. The problem is when we rely on a few particular sources for information we limit our scope because, without other sources to confirm or round out information, we rely on a viewpoint that is narrowed.

Media sound bites create an abbreviated glimpse into a culture, religion, race, or issue. These rumors, generalizations, and speculation can be detrimental to our society. Evidence of this was observed after the events of 9/11, as perceptions of Islam and the cultures of Afghanistan and Iraq were played out in media snippets, causing many to fear and retaliate against American Muslims.

Our defense is to think critically about what the media is portraying, to not take the information at face value, to inquire about what questions were unanswered and what points of view weren't presented, and to seek out additional sources of information without relying on a selected few favorites.

CULTIVATION THEORY

As we become more dependent on the media, the greater media portrayals become a reality. Beginning in the 1960s, George Gerbner proposed that over time our exposure to media messages "cultivates" our perceptions of reality. This cultivated reality is not achieved after a simple viewing of a program or film, but is cumulative in nature in that over time our values and attitudes are formed based on repetitive media messages, particularly that of television; as a result our behaviors may be modified.

Given our media diet of crime shows, which include scripted shows such as *Blue Bloods*, the various versions of *NCIS* and *Law & Order,* as well as reality shows, the average view of crime is that it is increasing dramatically when in fact it has been decreasing steadily. Gerbner called this the "mean world syndrome,"[3] where we perceive the world to be a much more dangerous place than it actually is.

We must realize that the world the media constructs is not the most realistic. Gerbner went on to say that the media is a cultural storyteller. That where once we learned about our society and our place in it from our families, churches, and schools, we now learn this from the media often well before we enter kindergarten. The media then contributes to the construction and maintenance of our culture based on what we see and hear. It is indeed an unofficial curriculum developing our manners, values, morals, and attitudes. While we often reflect what the media offers us through our behaviors, we sometimes see it reflected back at us in the themes and storylines of the media.

Narcotizing Dysfunction

With our ever-growing diet of media, we are bombarded with information on issues and concerns on a continual basis. The consequence is that the effect is narcotizing. We become numb or desensitized to the information and therefore the issue. We become apathetic to social and political matters. This in turn makes us dysfunctional, unable or unwilling to devote time to take action. Worse yet, we think we are involved simply because of the knowledge that was attained through the media.

These theories serve to illustrate the psychological power the media has in influencing us in our perceptions, attitudes, and values, but also the power that we have given to it as a result of allowing media to become a commanding influence in our lives.

◉ MEDIA IS BIG BUSINESS

Following significant mergers in the 1980s, major media businesses began to pressure the government for deregulation. Media ownership was strictly regulated limiting the amount of media outlets that a company could own to a mere handful and the trend was toward locally owned and operated radio and television stations and newspapers. At the time, broadcasting companies could own no more than 20 radio stations nationwide. Today iHeartMedia, is the nation's largest radio broadcasting companies, with over 850 stations in over 150 markets across the country.[4] Where once a company could only own a few radio or television stations nationwide, today a handful of large conglomerates own the majority of the media we watch, listen to, and read. Many argue that this concentration of ownership has resulted in less diversity, as there are fewer voices and points of view, a decline of quality programming and an increase in formulaic creations, and greater power being wielded by so few.

Another ramification of deregulation is that these media conglomerates often do not own a single source of media, such as film or television, rather they own various elements of the media industry to include print publications, recording labels, distribution companies, and even exhibition venues in which to display their media products. This level of cross-media ownership has intensified and can be scrutinized by examining some of the large media entities.

⊚ TRENDS IN MEDIA OWNERSHIP

CROSS-MEDIA OWNERSHIP

The Federal Communications Commission (FCC) is the federal regulatory agency that is responsible for "implementing and upholding America's communication laws and regulations" which includes media ownership.[5]

In 1996, one of the first major changes in over six decades occurred with the Telecommunications Act which allowed for major deregulation of the media industry. Ownership exploded with the passage of the act, as companies were allowed to extend outside of their normal operations. Media companies had far fewer restrictions, not only in terms of the number of outlets they could own, but also they were no longer limited to one form of media. Broadcasting companies could own both radio and television stations, for example, and telephone companies could become Internet service providers. With that the trend turned away from a few home-grown media outlets toward chains, networks, and major media conglomerates.[6]

While there are still some ownership limitations, primarily measured by market share, the number of media outlets a company can own has swelled. Much of the deregulation that occurred was due to industry pressure on the regulatory agencies that govern them. Since the Telecommunications Act of 1996 was passed, several media companies became conglomerates, and have since used their power to pressure for even further deregulation.

The FCC further relaxed cross-media ownership rules in 2017, by permitting TV and radio station owners to acquire a daily newspaper in the same market increasing the types of media outlets any one entity can own in a single market.[7]

Media regulations do limit the number of TV and radio stations a company can own in a market. Radio ownership is decided using a sliding scale. In large markets with 45 or more stations, a single company can own up to eight stations, while in a smaller market of 14 or less stations, a company can own five.[8]

Local television ownership is limited to two stations within the same market but with very stringent parameters, though some owners like Sinclair Broadcasting have pushed these limits, violating the regulations. Sinclair has a history of regulatory infringements, and in 2020 they were fined a record breaking $45 million for not only knowingly violating the regulations but also for their deceptive reporting to the FCC.[9]

LIMITED COMPETITION AND POWER

As a result, there are far fewer owners, and far less diversity. This state of limited competition is called an oligopoly and generates inherent concerns.

As media conglomerates have been allowed to grow in size due to mergers and acquisitions they also gain in the power they can exert. Concentrated ownership, in the hands of a few, provides fewer points of view, a potentially limited value system, and a greater base of power. As the gatekeepers of information, this power has been exerted to prohibit or censor the voices of others and to create partisanship toward their agenda or political bias. The term "fake news" has been bantered about, by political candidates, those in office, and the parties that represent them because the reporting of certain media outlets did not align with their perspective. There are certainly news outlets on either side of the political spectrum as well as owners with personal values and ethics that they exercise through their media holdings–all of which are in direct opposition to the main principles of the Journalistic Code of Ethics that states that "ethical journalism should be accurate and fair."[10]

Limited competition also suggests that there is a smaller playing field in the media market, which is better for the company as it has a greater chance to dominate, but also suggests that there might be less of something else. A media market devoid of competitors is a very difficult market to work with or to work in.

With fewer owners controlling more of the area advertising venues there are less choices of advertising rates and packaging programs. The lack of advertising competition is not the only effect. As media groups merge, they pool their resources, which can be a benefit for the corporation but a detriment to the employees. It is now harder to break into the industry, and there are significantly fewer jobs, as companies combine their operations including their staffs. One office suite may now house the broadcast operations for several radio stations allowing them to share equipment and personnel.

Many media companies do not concentrate on a few forms of media, rather they choose to create a corporation that combines various entities from media or media-related industries as well as non-media holdings whose power increases with their growing portfolios.

There are only a handful of major conglomerates that own most of the media outlets in the United States. Their vast assets make them powerful players in media and beyond. This point can be best illustrated by looking at two of the major media entities, the Walt Disney Company (Disney) and News Corporation (News Corp).

Disney is perhaps best known for their most valuable non-media enterprise—their parks and resorts—and certainly we are familiar with Disney films. Both are enormous assets, but their media holdings go much further. Disney also controls several other film studios, including Pixar, the more recently required 20th Century Studios, and Searchlight Pictures, the American Broadcasting Company (ABC) television network, and several cable networks, including ESPN. The company also owns recording labels, crosses over into print media with magazines and book publishers, and less visible forms of the media industry such as distribution companies. Beyond the media there are retail shops, cruise lines, and theatrical productions.[11]

News Corp's founder, Rupert Murdoch, started as a newspaper mogul in his native Australia. Upon growing his empire there, he turned to media in the United States, changing his citizenship to accommodate American restrictions on foreign ownership. While News Corp has established an extensive foundation in publishing through Harper Collins book publishers, and a worldwide base in newspapers, including the *New York Post* and the *Wall Street Journal*, until recently the company had also controlled several film studios, and, the Fox broad-cast broadcasting network, and cable networks.[12] However, in 2017, the Murdoch family decided to reconfigure selling 20th Century Film Studios to Disney and separating the Fox Broadcasting Network and TV stations into a separate company shared with Disney. [13]

These examples are just a sample of the ever changing media land-scape and the means to which media conglomerates squire and merge their assets.

VERTICAL INTEGRATION

When a single media company achieves a high level of cross-media ownership, in order to control several aspects of the industry, they have attained vertical integration. In the previous examples the conglomerates own the means to produce media through their various studios, can deliver the media product through their distribution services, and can exhibit that product via broadcast television and cable networks, at venues in their theme parks, and at company-owned theaters. This integration of media entities allows a company to maintain control of the product from production through distribution to the consumer, and reap the profits.

SYNERGY

The ability for a company to combine the various efforts described above is called synergy. Using the multiple companies that a conglomerate owns within various media industries to promote media products is a key advantage to cross-media ownership. A conglomerate can produce a film at one of their studios, then advertise the theater opening through their print media, radio, television, and outdoor advertising companies. However, promotional approaches go beyond advertising as articles can be written for the print publications detailing an interesting aspect of the film such as an innovative technique used in filming, an interview with a prominent cast member, or a photo essay highlighting the location in which the film was shot. Television specials can chronicle the making of the film, the stars of the film appear on multiple talk shows, trailers for the film appear on the Internet and in the theaters, and merchandise tie-ins are peddled through retail stores and theme parks.

The effect of media synergy is that by combining efforts, the media product develops a much greater impact than it could have if promoted separately.

GLOBALIZATION

Disney and News Corp, as well as other media giants like Time-Warner, have taken their vast resources beyond the boundaries of the United States. Even Virginia-based, Gannett Newspapers owns 102 daily papers, and 1200 non-dailies worldwide, and has entered into television ownership as well.[14]

Many other media companies, like Sony and Bertelsmann, started overseas and combined their massive holdings with stateside mergers.

⊚ THE MEDIA IS IN BUSINESS TO PROFIT

Although many people believe that the primary function of the media is information and entertainment, like any business, the media is in business to make money, and media revenue is generated primarily through advertising. While subscribers generate some of the revenue for print media, for cable and satellite television or radio, it is the number of viewers or listeners who determine the greatest revenue stream. Higher circulation and ratings figures entice advertisers as they know they will receive a greater return on their investment. Advertising costs are usually measured on what it costs per thousand viewers or readers. For example, an ad costing $20,000 to run in a magazine with a total circulation of 2,950,000 readers would cost $6.78 per thousand readers. The greater number of readers the more economical the advertisement is to run. However, when readership declines, or the number of viewers of a television program decreases, the publication can be in jeopardy of folding or the television show may be canceled.

It is therefore important for each medium to generate increased interest in order to produce considerable circulation or ratings numbers.

AGENDA SETTING

The media has the power to present the events of the day, and to make us aware of issues or concerns and their consequences. However, what is chosen to air is left to the gatekeepers, those editors and producers of the media who have the authority to decide what stories to release and how. The media then has the ability to tell the public what issues are important based on what they choose to highlight. If the media reports on declining graduation rates or rising numbers of mortgage defaults, then we believe the issues must have some significance, because the stories were important enough for the media to report on. This can generate an increased concern among the public, even if it wasn't a concern prior to the media exposure.

Given all of the possible issues and concerns, the media gatekeepers must also decide what stories to run in the limited space that they have. For instance, the local news has a limited time slot, but in that time they must cover national headlines as well as the local weather and sports leaving a minimal amount of time to deliver the local news. Choices must then be made about what media packages to run, for how long, and in what order. The stories are prioritized with the lead story generating the most interest among the public, but not necessarily impacting the most people. Often these can include local disasters, such as fires or accidents, or a controversial topic. Even the news is constructed to draw in an audience.

That brings us to a primary concern. If the media chooses to cover stories and issues because that will bring in an audience, are they are choosing what is important to know or what will result in larger ratings?

FORMULAIC MEDIA THEMES

We've heard the phrase "if it isn't broke don't fix it." When television programming or movie themes have proven successful, the media often maintains that theme creating sequels, spin-offs, and copycat versions. It has been said that there are only seven different categories for plot lines in books, television, and film and the media capitalizes on these and there previous successes.

For example, many prosperous television shows have led to spin-offs including the many versions within the *Law & Order* and *NCIS* franchises.

Film sequels abound with multiples of *Transformers, The Lord of the Rings, Men in Black, the Fast & the Furious, Pirates of the Caribbean, The Matrix,* and *Toy Story,* just to name a few. Movie themes are also perpetuated through characters such as *James Bond, Indiana Jones,* and *Austin Powers,* and the variety of characters made popular through the DC and Marvel series from the *X-Men* to *Captain America* and *Batman.*

Books have used serial characters since the Civil War, creating a succession of books that create a following of readers. Certainly the *Harry Potter*, *Twilight*, and *Hunger Games* series are examples of series that crossed over from successful books to successful films.

Recording labels also follow trends, signing artists with a commercial sound that has already proven successful and they need to ride the trend of the times. We have seen different variations of boy bands and solo blonds but as audiences tired of the sameness and streaming services allowed us to create our own playlists audiences explored more. There are less predominate genres of music now as there are more cross over hits like *"Old Town Road"* and even resurging hits from decades ago like Queen's *"Bohemian Rhapsody."*

Radio stations follow this tendency as well, although it is often tied to the concentration of ownership. Because a broadcasting company may own several stations across the country, a cost-effective arrangement is to have those that play the same format, such as Top 40 or adult contemporary, use the same promotional campaigns, the same "phrase that pays," and the same slogan. In some cases the station is not a physical entity at all, but a computer server playing a canned playlist with prerecorded local spots interjected from time to time.

Even news coverage has become formulaic; in fact we expect it. We look for certain information to be packaged with a story—an auto accident, for example—where we would expect certain shots at the scene such as images of the wreck, victims being tended to, a long shot of the street, and interviews of witnesses or first responders.

The reason for this formulaic blueprint is that it is cost effective. Much can be gained off a successful original, as sequels tend to bring in more at the box office than their predecessors. Television spin-offs offer much to a network as well, because the new show is likely to draw an audience from the loyal following of the original show, just as books carry devoted readers through a series. It is also productive for a media company to have a set of standard practices that can be used throughout their many media holdings, streamlining marketing campaigns for use in multiple outlets, and achieving a high level of expectations for the employees and consumers alike.

⬤ EMBEDDED VALUES AND POINTS OF VIEW

So far the dominance of the media in our lives has been stressed at various points in this book, and this chapter has presented media theories introducing several ways in which the media can influence us. This section offers another means in which the media has influence over an audience in its ability to create and perpetuate certain values and points of view. This is significant in that we have learned that the media can cultivate a reality based on the information disseminated from media messages, and that these messages are perpetuated via the repetitiveness of formulaic programming.

BIAS

While journalistic ethics call for the reporting of truth in an objective manner, there are certain media publications, programs, and websites that have a decisive slant to their coverage. Progressive points of view have been the mainstay of radio programming on Air America Radio, while conservative commentators tout views on the other side of the political spectrum. While these examples of radio programming are obvious in their stance, not all media outlets are. As discussed earlier, some media outlets will choose to enhance particular attitudes in an effort to persuade or bolster opinions, while limiting dissenting viewpoints. It is then imperative that we identify any source of information and determine their agenda before taking it at face value, and we need to rely on multiple sources for a well-rounded perspective.

OMISSIONS AND MARGINALIZATION

Any constructed message is pieced together to communicate meaning. No news program can cover all of the news of the day, no photographer can take in every angle of a scene, and every point of view can't be addressed. Therefore, we must understand that something is always being omitted and then try to detect the exclusion. Perhaps there are voices and viewpoints that aren't being heard or concerns that aren't being addressed. To omit these voices is to silence segments of our society that have every right to be heard.

The list of marginalized groups is long, from the more general groups that include women, non-whites, and non-Christians to the homeless, immigrants, the LGBTQ community, veterans, the elderly, teens aged out of foster care, as well as those living with disabilities or in poverty. Society in general, and mainstream media specifically, tend not to acknowledge these groups and therefore overlook their needs, beliefs, and concerns. Occasionally there will be a news story, a special report, or an individual that is included as a character in an ensemble cast. Shows like the *7 Little Johnston's* or *My 600 Pound Life* may demonstrate the lives certain individuals lead, but some criticize these shows as more spectacle than insightful.

Though we are beginning to see representations of more diversity in media, it is certainly not the norm, and much more often these groups are either invisible or exaggerated. Such misrepresentation leads to stereotyping.

STEREOTYPES

As discussed in an earlier chapter, generalizations are necessary to create a greater level of understanding for a large audience. However, there is an inherent danger in depicting a narrow set of values or limiting points of view. Generalizations often create a stereotype of a person or concept, resulting in a rather limited perspective. Stereotypes often infer certain characteristics about groups of people, leading to

categorization by generation, ethnicity, gender, sexual orientation, and even by occupation. The danger occurs when our perceptions of reality are shaped by these narrowed media perspectives.

Stereotypes are created and sustained in the media by limiting character choices in film and television roles. Typecasting minority actors as servants, alcoholics, or gang members can "perpetuate social prejudice and inequality" [16] while a lack of diversity among characters does not accurately reflect our culture, and serves to prolong the image of white superiority.

Behaviors are often stereotypically associated with people of certain races and sexual orientations. This may include mannerisms or gestures, speech patterns, and even hairstyles and clothing.

Gender stereotyping perpetuates the images of men and women in the media, where women are expected to be feminine, nurturing caregivers, and men the masculine providers. Even expectations for body image have some rather unrealistic expectations for both genders, and for those individuals that do not identify with any specific gender–they are overlooked .

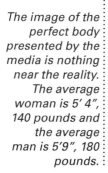

The image of the perfect body presented by the media is nothing near the reality. The average woman is 5' 4", 140 pounds and the average man is 5'9", 180 pounds.

Body Image and the Media

As a society, we have unrealistic expectations of body image that is based on pervasive media depictions. Unfortunately, that ideal image aligns more closely with that of fashion models than the average American male or female.

The average female runway model is 5'9" tall and weighs between 100-120 pounds. Male models average 5'11–6'2", 150 pounds and fit.[16] Yet the tall, slender, well-endowed female ever present in the media does not compare to the national average of the 5'4" woman weighing approximately 170 pounds and wearing a size 14.[17] Nor does the beefy male of the fashion catalog measure up to the average American male who is 5' 9" tall and weighs approximately 198 pounds.[18]

There is more to these numbers than just the staggering disparity between the media depictions and reality. While the average American's height has remained unchanged, both males and females are heavier. In 10 years, the average for women has increased by 30 pounds and men have gained an average of 18 pounds. According to the CDC, the new averages, for both males and females, would be categorized as overweight. It is no wonder that our health care professionals are after us to take greater care with our health as obesity rates have continued to rise.[19]

But there is even more to the continuing disillusionment as it pertains to size. While it is widely reported that the average woman is a size 14–she is not. Ten years ago, the average woman was a 140 pounds and a size 14, so how could she gain 30 pounds and still wear the same size? In fact, the average woman is closer to a size 16 or 18, unless the manufacturers adjusted their clothing sizes–which they did.

Sizing standards for women's clothing was first developed in the 1940s with the rather limited criteria of bust size. Though the criteria has been adjusted over the years, the average overall woman's size increased, and manufacturers began to practice "vanity sizing" because what was once an 8 became a 14. Sensitive to their clientele, manufacturers adjusted their larger sizes numerically downward because "women don't want to know their real size." [20] As a result of these adjustments, smaller sizes needed to be added and in 2011, the addition of size 0 and 00 clothing was added.[21] Though we are bombarded by the unrealistic expectations of body image there is also a dichotomy of expectations between what men and women actually prefer. Women believe the ideal is closer to the model– tall, thin, larger breasts–while men actually prefer their women with more curves. Women chose men with toned, athletic builds while the men thought women would prefer a physique that was much more muscular with bulked up biceps, thighs, and ripped abs. Perhaps we need to talk to each other more.

Glamour Magazine agrees, as they have published results from a variety of surveys regarding how men interpret the female ideal. According to a 2012 survey, "78% of the men surveyed said they would rather date a confident plus-size woman that an insecure supermodel" and the part of the body that they preferred most is probably not what you would think–the "whole package" came in at number one with the derrière a close second.[22]

So how can our perceptions be so wrong? This misconception of body shape starts in childhood, with toys such as Barbie and G.I.Joe. Barbie's proportions are so unrealistic, that if she were a real person she would be seven feet tall and fall over from her top-heavy frame and her too small feet.[23] The biceps of G.I.Joe have been steadily increasing to an unrealistic dimension.[24] This unrealistic perception of body image continues through adolescence and into adulthood with exposure to a variety of media in which the portrayal of the body is both unrealistic and unattainable.

These implausible images have led to an overwhelming dissatisfaction with physical appearance among men and women, and has caused eating disorders in both

genders to rise. Because of the depictions of the body in the media, women are trying to slim down, men are eliminating body hair and trying to bulk up, because muscles are perceived as masculine and body hair is unsightly. Both sexes often use methods that are hazardous to their health to achieve these unrealistic expectations, and eating disorders such as anorexia and bulimia are rising among both men and women.

The bottom line is that the media is misleading us regarding its representations of body image, our childhood toys captivated us, clothing manufacturers have been tricking us into thinking we have not added pounds, we perceive each other inaccurately, and now if this wasn't enough–we mislead ourselves. Several universities have conducted studies that posit that the more time spent on social media the more likely we are to be depressed and to be more dissatisfied with our body image.[25]

One company that has tried to change the perception of body image, is Dove by Unilever, who specializes in skin and hair care products. They began to use "real women, not professional models, of various ages, shapes, and sizes" when they launched their "Campaign for Real Beauty" in 2004. They have continued with variations of this theme since, through the Self-Esteem Project and Project Show Me campaign.[26]

While Dove's campaigns are quite admirable and has triggered much discussion, until the media and fashion industries make a significant change to the representation of the body, these media messages will continue to be unrealistic and misleading.

◉ MEDIA DEVELOPMENT

There are various forms of media, each with a rich developmental history, and operating characteristics specific to them. Every form of media has advanced with the latest developments in technology, even embracing them by converging with them.

NEWSPAPERS

Newspapers began as simple news sheets in the colonial era that were posted in town and printed only occasionally. These early papers eventually became dailies, and served as the primary source of news and information. Papers flourished into the 1800s, often with multiple papers in metropolitan areas resulting in intensified competition.

Early papers lacked visual interest and, in fact, had little visual structure. The visual hierarchy was primarily textual, although an occasional illustrative image would be used. Illustrations were the mainstay of imagery until the first photograph was printed in a periodical in 1873 with the development of the halftone. A halftone allows a photograph to be reproduced by reducing the image to a series of dots. This technology is stilled used today to reproduce images in any print medium. By looking closely at any printed image with a magnifying glass one can see the obvious dot pattern. The name is derived from the fact that when reduced to dots the image loses half its tonal range essentially and literally becoming a halftone.

Papers can be divided into many categories including weeklies, shoppers, and even a variety of dailies. Dailies are characterized by information divided into sections. National dailies are papers written and distributed for a national audience like the *Wall Street Journal* and the *USA Today.*

The *Wall Street Journal* is one of the oldest papers in the United States, founded by Charles Dow and Edward Jones in 1889. Clarence Barron then purchased control of the paper in 1902. It is best known for its in-depth articles focusing on world business and finance. The paper has had a very traditional and text heavy structure, until a series of redesigns starting in 2002 integrated subtle color

and narrowed the paper by eliminating a column. However, the *Wall Street Journal* still holds to its more traditional style for their front page. In December 2007, the *Wall Street Journal* was purchased by Rupert Murdoch (News Corp), ending 79 years of family ownership by the Bancroft family, the descendants of Clarence Barron.

Newspapers were heavily impacted by the introduction of television, which offered news in an interesting and highly visual format. *USA Today* was introduced in 1982 by the Gannett Company, the largest newspaper chain in the United States. Originally designed for business travelers, the paper features brief, easy-to-read stories on the go. The format was designed to emulate television in a print format with the extensive use of color, photographs, infographics, and short articles similar to the television sound-bite.

This highly visual paper has been fervently criticized for its soft approach to news, earning the nickname the "McPaper" by journalists who believe the image-heavy design and articles written at a middle school level are "dumbing down" the news. Although it has been highly criticized, it has proved to be a commercial success. With a daily circulation of over 2.8 million, it is the paper with the largest circulation in the United States.

Metro dailies are the local daily papers that are written and distributed for a regional municipality, with a focus on regional news. Where once several papers may have thrived in a metropolitan area, most cities are served today by only one daily paper. Although many adults receive their news from sources like television and radio, the newspaper is able to provide in-depth information including details about the event, background information, and examinations of the impact on the community.

Metro dailies are also characterized by zoned editions often for different geographical territories. The *Democrat and Chronicle (D&C)* is an example of the metro daily paper for Rochester, New York, and the surrounding region. It is also a Gannett paper, and one of the oldest in the Gannett portfolio.

Most cities have a rather mixed audience and the structure of the average daily follows with a mix of image and text. While not as colorful and vibrant as *USA Today* metro dailies usually feature large attention getting front page images, multiple headlines, infographics, and advertising.

As one of the main sources of local news, it is not surprising that it is also a major source of local advertising; in fact, "advertisers spend as much in print advertising as they do in desktop Internet ads" [27]

Because papers are a tangible, trusted source of information, and readers trust print ads more than those in other media,[28] they are an attractive venue for advertising. Newspapers depend on advertising as their primary source of revenue.

Front page of Rochester Democrat & Chronicle, 10/10/20

The *D&C* and the *USA Today* are two of the 90 dailies Gannett owns in the United States as well as the Newsquest Media Group in the United Kingdom.

Until recently, the company's holdings did not end with newspapers, as Gannett owned broadcast television stations, and several websites, including CareerBuilder. However, in 2015, the company separated its companies between the newspaper and publishing group and the newly formed Tegna, Inc., represents broadcast and digital media.[29] In 2019, the parent company of Gatehouse Media acquired Gannett, yet maintained the Gannett name.[30]

Many are troubled by the fact that most local papers have lost their regional control as they are now owned, and continually acquired by, larger media corporations with transient executives who swoop in and out of a city, on their way up the corporate ladder.

But the newspaper industry has also struggled as they fell victim to their own poor business models. As commercial websites and social media took hold, the newspaper industry gave away their product for free, and soon consumers began to drop their subscriptions. Years later, newspapers addressed the issue with a pay wall, but by then the damage was done and many consumers were looking for free sources of information.

MAGAZINES

Colonial magazines were sporadic in their publication, until mass circulation was achieved in the 1800s after the Civil War. Unlike the regional reach of newspapers, magazines had a national audience creating a commonality among readers nationwide, and perhaps of more consequence, a national platform for advertising.

Most magazines were classified as general-interest magazines containing articles that had widespread appeal. Among the most popular of this category was the *Saturday Evening Post,* which began publication in 1821 as a newspaper and was redesigned as a magazine in 1898.The *Post,* like other general-interest magazines, reflected on society by featuring articles on issues of interest, short well-written pieces of fiction, and even serialized novels by top authors. The *Saturday Evening Post* was published for 148 years, and was probably best known for the more than 300 covers created by Norman Rockwell in a span of 50 years.

Several restarts to the Post were attempted including a term as a special-interest magazine with a focus on health and medical information until its current reiteration, back to a general interest magazine. It is published six times a year by the Saturday Evening Post Society.[31]

Magazines developed from the mid-1880s into the 1900s by seeking new audiences and tailoring their content to them. Special-interest magazines were created for niche audiences with specifically focused content. The largest area of expansion were magazines developed specifically for women, but many other interest areas soon followed. Magazines were developed to explore the arts, literature, political commentary, and more.

In 1923 Henry Luce created Time, with an emphasis on news and current events, followed in 1925 by Harold Ross who published The New Yorker, which focused on art and literature. Both are still published today.

As magazines became more popular, they became more competitive and sought new approaches to developing a following. Both *Life* and *Look* magazines were considered general-interest magazines, but their large format was particularly

suited to their distinctive focus on photojournalism. Their iconic photos serve as a chronicle of American history and culture. Although neither remain today, catalogs of their comprehensive photos can be found online. When *Look* folded, the extensive image collection was donated to the Library of Congress.

McClure's started in 1893 as a literary magazine, but repositioned itself with an emphasis on investigative reporting in 1902. Perhaps best known for Ida Tarbell's piece on the corporate abuses of the Standard Oil Company, the style became known as muckraking journalism. The magazine folded in 1929.

Ladies Home Journal was first published in 1883. As a women's magazine, it was known for its crusades for public health and women's role in society. In 1929, the magazine uncovered the truth behind the then-unregulated patent medicines which were found to contain large amounts of alcohol, opium, and morphine and sold to unknowing consumers. The exposure eventually led to the passage of the Federal Pure Food and Drug Act.[32] The magazine ended publication in 2016.

With changing audiences as well as the introduction of television, the demise of general-interest magazines was inevitable. Many general-interest magazines have folded and special-interest publications now dominate the market. The number of magazines carried at newsstands, bookstores, and supermarkets has grown immensely with far-ranging subjects and titles from *Golf* to *Cigar Aficionado*.

A distinct characteristic of magazine publishing is the addition of display ads, which correlate to the magazine's niche and target audience. Advertising is an important revenue stream for the magazine industry, and most consumers state that they find magazines to be more relevant to them and trust the information and advertising found within them. [33] This is not surprising, as readers often choose a special interest publication that aligns with their interests.

The number of magazines has remained fairly stable since 2002 with several new launches in 2018 in both food, and the health and wellness categories.[34]

Magazines appeal to Americans of all ages, and serve a very diverse audience, with 91% of adults having read a magazine in the past 6 months. Perhaps more surprising was the fact that 94% of those adults were under 25.[35] Though competition from digital media is strong, magazines have embraced digital and social media, creating synergy among the various media entities.

RADIO

The origination of wireless telegraphy, or radio, has been contested for years between Nikola Tesla and Guglielmo Marconi. Both made significant contributions to the development of radio with their work, but it was Marconi who registered the first patents beginning in 1898, creating the Wireless Telegraph Company and promoting his work publicly. Marconi demonstrated the first real impact of radio technology by outfitting sea going ships with radio, permitting ship-to-shore communication for the first time in history. However, it was Tesla who the U.S. Supreme Court recognized as the inventor of radio in 1943, finding Marconi's patents invalid because they were originally developed by Tesla.

Early radio could only transmit code until 1906 when Reginald Fessenden and Lee Deforest discovered how to adjust electromagnetic waves to human voice. Fessenden transmitted the first live broadcast and an entertainment medium was born. Both claimed the patent rights and wound up tying each other up in court. Various other companies such as American Marconi, General Electric, American Telephone and Telegraph (AT&T), and Westinghouse controlled patents to vital technology. The inability to cooperate and share the technology inhibited the advancement of radio. In 1919 the U.S. government forced a merger during World War I to accelerate the production of radio for the war effort. What was created as a result of this government-sanctioned monopoly was the Radio Corporation of America (RCA) with the purpose of maintaining American control of radio. General Electric led the newly formed cooperative because it was their transmitters that would pave the way for radio to become a powerful medium.

Government involvement continued through regulation, delineating a real separation in media, because print media is not regulated by any government agency to this day. The Wireless Ship Act of 1910 required ships to have a wireless radio and an operator on board. Stricter shipboard operations were initiated after the Titanic disaster when the radio operators of nearby ships were asleep, missing the frantic calls of the Titanic's operator. The Radio Act of 1912 required ships to have on-duty operators at all times, and for the first time individual stations had to be licensed and were issued frequencies on which to operate. Those not adhering to the regulations were fined. Legal challenges to the regulations forced President Coolidge to deregulate and chaos ensued.

Further regulation created the Federal Radio Commission as the regulatory agency over radio and reinstated the issuance of licenses, frequencies, and fines. Later the agency became the Federal Communications Commission, which regulates both radio and television today. Most importantly broadcasters do not own the channels on which they operate; they operate in the public's interest and as such are subject to content regulations.

The first radio station was created by Westinghouse as a means to sell receivers. However, once receivers became a mainstay in many homes, radio stations turned to advertising as a source of revenue. The first radio ads were accepted in 1922, and soon after advertisers realized the potential of a mass national audience and created the programming, ushering in the era of "The Golden Age of Radio." Programming consisted of nightly music programs with symphonies, big bands, opera music, and the Grand Ole Opry, as well as variety shows, drama series, quiz shows, and comedies.

In 1926 RCA created the first network of interconnected stations known as the National Broadcasting Company (NBC). RCA launched a second network in 1927 after acquiring AT&T stations. The two networks were simply designated internally as the red and blue networks. The Columbia Broadcasting System (CBS) followed in 1929 and the Mutual Broadcasting System in 1934. However by 1941, the FCC determined that NBC had a dominant stance

in American broadcasting and was ordered to sell off one of the networks. The choice was to sell off the blue network, which then became the American Broadcasting Company (ABC).

Radio programming took a devastating blow with the introduction of television. Advertisers began to flock to the new medium, adjusting their radio shows to the visual format of television, leaving radio stations without content. Searching for an inexpensive way to fill airtime, radio stations turned to recorded music. After first incurring fines for royalty infractions, the radio industry developed the means to collect royalties for artists, a system that remains in place today.

With the content shift to recorded music came the need to specialize, as specific audiences are attracted to certain kinds of music. This aided the advertisers who could focus on niche audiences and was the beginning of format radio, where a station plays a specific genre of music such as country, adult contemporary, Top 40, Christian, or an all news format.

Most stations transmitted on the AM band until the frequencies were exhausted in the 1960s. FM stations began to evolve as alternative music and messaging of the time sought airtime. The shift to FM continued through the 1970s, particularly once it was realized that the wider signal of FM resulted in better sound quality and the ability to broadcast in stereo. It is for this reason that most music stations broadcast on FM frequencies and AM stations have shifted to formats such as talk, news, and sports.

The radio industry also fell victim to the concentration of ownership. Further changes resulted from acquisitions and mergers, and all four of the major networks from the Golden Age of Radio no longer exist. The Mutual Broadcasting System underwent several changes of ownership, and was purchased by radio powerhouse Westwood One, who later purchased the NBC radio network and was then acquired by Cumulus Media in 2013. Cumulus already owned the former ABC radio network. CBS was sold to Entercom in 2017, thus ending the era of radio powerhouses that had been associated with major television networks.

Radio is also no stranger to newer forms of competition, with streaming services that offer everything from customized playlists, to podcasts covering a variety of topics. Despite this, radio is steady across all major demographics and reaches 95% of American adults.[36] Today, iHeartMedia is the industry leader, with over 850 stations across the United States. They have embraced the digital age offering audio in various formats including the traditional broadcast radio, podcasts and a free app for consumers that integrates all of these platforms.[37]

MOTION PICTURES

Motion pictures developed from simple influences, such as the flip book and zoetropes. Both use a series of still pictures that vary slightly so that, when the pages are flipped through in rapid succession, there is an illusion of movement. This idea of animating still images was advanced when in 1877 race horse owner Leland Stanford decided to settle a long-standing dispute about whether at full gallop a horse's hooves come completely off the ground at the same time. He hired photographer Eadweard Muybridge to capture the action thereby hoping to settle the debate. By  placing a series of still cameras around a horse track and outfitting them with trip wires, a series of images were created as the horse tripped the shutter of each camera. The result was a study of motion, which did indeed prove that a horse does have all four hooves off the ground at one time.

Muybridge continued these studies of animals in motion and presented his images using a zoopraxiscope, a device that placed the drawings of images on a glass disc, much like a record, which when rotated and illuminated from behind, appeared to create moving images. This display is said to have influenced William Dickson of Edison Laboratories who created the first celluloid strip of images. Edison went on to introduce the Kinetoscope, which allowed a single user to view a continuous loop of celluloid film through a viewer. These early films were also primarily studies in motion, someone skipping rope, juggling, even sneezing.

It was however Europeans who developed the first projection systems for group viewings and also the first motion picture camera. Most nota-

bly among these were brothers Auguste and Louis Lumière. Edison soon followed with a projection system called the Vitascope. Years of patent disputes followed until eventually Edison led the group to form a cooperative, essentially an industry monopoly, called the Motion Picture Patents Company, nicknamed "the Trust." The group essentially held all patents for every aspect of the film industry, from production through exhibition, and dictated strict and very limiting means of film production. One of the members of the Trust was the Eastman Kodak Company, though their only interest was to supply film to the members. Eventually the Trust was dismantled as a result of a Supreme Court decision, but by then extensive changes to the film industry had already occurred.

Independent film producers rebelled against the strict limits of the Trust, and began moving to California where there was more land to create studios and outdoor sets, the ability to film in a more conducive climate, and to get away from the grip of the Trust. Films developed from single reels and studies of motion to narrative films that told a story through plot lines and character development. However, the studios soon became powerhouses exerting their control over various aspects of the industry. Studios developed stars and controlled them through iron-clad contracts. Then they gained vertical integration by gaining enough power and control of the industry to produce and distribute films, and to exert power over theater owners. Although this power was eventually broken up by a Supreme Court decision, it served to once again create a surge of independent film production.

The film industry has experienced a rich history of different eras characterized by advances in technology from silent films to the introduction of sound, and then color, to 3-D technology, and the growing sophistication of special effects. Influences outside the industry also impacted the production of film, like the public outcry over content, which resulted in the industry's self-regulation beginning in 1934 with the "Production Code." The strict guidelines outlined by the Code led to the musicals and comedies of the "Golden Age of Film." Later the Code was replaced by the ratings system, which gave filmmakers more freedom to explore different themes.

The ratings system remains in place today, although the ratings of G, PG, PG-13, R, and NC-17 are the third generation of that system.

Another outside influence that had an enormous impact on the film industry is the introduction of television. Once visual entertainment entered people's own homes, the film industry was met with heavy competition, which only increased with the advent of cable and premium movie channels like HBO and Showtime. Today, box office receipts do not account for the bulk of the revenue as most of their money is derived from merchandise tie-ins, DVD sales, and streaming services. The COVID-19 pandemic shuttered theaters, expedidited release to streaming services. While the film industry has evolved with more sophisticated imagery, character development, storylines, and special effects, it has also fallen victim to formulaic themes and the sequel mentality.

Still, film is a mass medium that is not only a form of entertainment but an artform that is arranged to communicate ideas and feelings. We study film to understand the intricacies involved in their creation, which in turn enhances the enjoyment of the medium. This double awareness is the key to visual literacy.

THE VISUAL LANGUAGE OF FILM

As we have discussed before in previous chapters, there is a language to media. Much of the language of film can be attributed to photography as there is a similarity to pictorial imagery. In film the art is called cinematography. The major difference between the two is that in film the camera can move with the subject while filming, creating a continuous series of images. With that ability comes an enormous amount of options and creativity. These same techniques outlined here can also be found in television and even television commercials.

Storyboards

Films begin with an idea that is transformed into a storyline with characters that are developed throughout. This information is incorporated into a screenplay or script, which outlines the dialogue, action, and camera instructions. The script is then mapped out visually through a storyboard. Storyboards correspond to a script and are a means to visualize that script. While it cannot contain every shot in the film, it will describe the major

sequencing points with a sketch of the shot, and information taken directly from the script including a description of the camera action, transition information, a written description of the shot, dialogue/narration, and music/sound effects. The storyboard helps the director to design the shots used in the film.

Film Structure

Films are generally arranged by acts. The three act film is a common means in which to tell the story. Act I is the set up and introduces us to the characters and the situation, Act II contains the conflict along with the obstacles the characters must overcome, while Act III reveals the resolution.

Films are further divided into shots, scenes, and sequences. A shot is a series of frames of continuous film that run without a break in that continuity. A shot can be held for a fraction of a second or much longer. A scene is a series of shots, using the same characters, which build the action of the film. A sequence is a series of scenes that are connected by an event.

Basic Film Shots

As with photography, there is a series of relationships between the camera and the subject. The first is the relationship of distance, and can be carried out as in photography with the various viewpoints such as the extreme long shot, long shot, medium shot, and close-ups including the extreme close-up. Many films use an establishing long shot as an opening shot. It places the subject in a context with a wide view of their surroundings or environment. The camera can then move in on the subject, via a medium shot or close-up, to introduce the character.

Camera Angles

The camera can also be positioned to take advantage of different camera angles to include low vantage points and aerial or overhead shots. (Refer to Chapter 6 for specifics on photographic style). It is important to remember that the film or video camera can, and should, move while filming. Amateur videographers tend to remain stationary and shoot at stationary objects, which can certainly make for boring subject matter.

Zoom

Another technique created by the camera is the zoom, which alters the focal point of the lens so that the camera can zoom in on a subject from a long shot to a close-up in one continuous shot or the reverse, zoom out from a close-up to a long shot.

Simple cuts are the most common transitions used. The camera merely captures a shifts from one subject to another.

TRANSITIONS

There are different techniques to move from one shot to another and to ensure continuity called transitions. Common transitions are the simple cut, fades, dissolves, superimpositions, and wipes.

Simple Cut

The simple cut is the act of joining of two shots together. As the most common transition, it is, as its name implies, a simple break or cut in the film to the next shot. For example, if filming two people talking, the camera will cut from one while speaking, then perhaps to them both, and then to the other.

Fade

Fades are also fairly common and are usually used to show a passage of time. The technique where the screen darkens or goes to black is called a fade-out, and the opposite effect where the screen starts black and gradually lightens to the scene is a fade-in. Fades are often used to open and close the film as well as major time shifts, as stated earlier.

Fades are common transitions. A fade-out illustrated here, where the screen gradually darkens to black, is often used to close a film or television show.

Dissolve

A dissolve is the act of layering a fade-out and a fade-in together. However, the screen never goes black. Instead, there is a blurring of the two images as they are seen simultaneously. It is used so as not to break tempo and may represent a passage of time or a psychological shift such as a flashback.

The images on this page illustrate how a dissolve works. The transition begins with the image of the old house. It gradually fades while the image of the new house fades in one fluid progression. The suggestion is that the two images are the same building and that a transformation took place over time.

Superimposition

A superimposition is similar to a dissolve in that the two images appear together on screen. However, rather than the continuing progression of the dissolve, the images are held together at an almost stationary point while layered over each other. This allows the audience to identify with both. Again, there is no break point, and the images are usually relationally linked. It is used often in flashbacks, to show a psychological link, or the passage of time.

Wipe

A wipe is a transition that often uses a line or item that runs across the screen replacing one image with another. As the line crosses the screen, a new image beneath the first is revealed. The film *Young Frankenstein* makes extensive use of this technique.

CAMERA MOVEMENT

Panning and Tilting

Unlike still photography, a motion picture camera can move to follow the subject's actions and the subject can move either toward or away from the camera while filming. Several techniques include tilting, panning, dolly or tracking shots, and crane shots. Tilting refers to the ability of the camera to film while tilting up or down; panning, taken from the word panoramic, is the ability of the camera to film while swinging horizontally.

Dolly or Tracking Shots

Dolly or tracking shots are used to film subjects in motion. The camera is placed on a cart that often travels along a track. The camera can then move toward the subject for a dramatic effect, or away

from the subject, but also can move alongside them. In the film *Forrest Gump,* a dolly shot was used when the leads Forrest and Jenny meandered through a field deep in conversation. The track was laid in a similar meandering fashion curving back and forth to be able to coincide with the actor's movements. Cameras are also placed on trucks and cars to capture the movement of other vehicles.

Crane Shots

Cranes are used to film overhead shots. The camera is positioned on a long telescoping arm, which can rise above and extend out from the action to achieve the overhead position. In extreme cases, the camera can be attached to drones or helicopters for aerial shots.

The methods described here are only a brief glimpse into film technique as there are so many more that whole books and even college classes are created to study them. What is important to realize is that, as audiences, we have come to expect many of these techniques even if we are unfamiliar with the terms applied to them. Much of this has to do with the craftsmanship of editing. Editing is the art of taking the individual shots and splicing them into scenes and then sequences to form the film. Because many films are not filmed from start to finish, this aspect of film making is both necessary and, when done well, seamless.

We expect the story to be told in a manner that flows from one plot point to the next with a high level of visual variety in all visual media such as film, television, and even commercials. We expect a variety of shots, with differing viewpoints, pieced together in a cohesive fashion. We don't even realize how much we expect this visual variety until we have been subjected to the home video of a friend's vacation or party where there are long continuous shots with little or no action. We are bored with the images in seconds because we have been trained by our exposure to film and television to expect multiple shots from multiple angles within seconds. Even a 30-second commercial can have more than 20 cuts in it. Editing also sets the tempo for the film. Long shots with slow transitions tell us a story while fast-paced cuts keep up with action sequences.

TELEVISION

As stated before, many of these same techniques used in film are utilized in television, yet there are many differences to the two. First of course, is the screen size. Despite the fact that our television screens are getting larger and projection systems allow the image to be displayed on a wall, neither can compare with the experience of a movie theater. With an even larger screen and stereo surround-sound, we are immersed into darkness so that the experience becomes enveloping. Second, the screen resolution for film is far better than television, which is why a film looks better in the theater than when we view it on television.

There are also advantages to television. There is an intimacy with television because it is far more personal than the movie theater. We can watch in the comfort of our homes sprawled on the couch in our pajamas if we desire. We can even pause the DVD or streaming services when the bathroom run becomes necessary or to go to the kitchen for a snack. However, there are distractions at home that we don't have at the theater—the family member who talks through the film, the dog who needs to go out, or that load of laundry that needs to be changed.

The television experience is ongoing. With the hundreds of channels we have available to us today, streaming services, and the 24-hour cycle of programming, there is always something to choose from. Television is still our primary medium for news and entertainment, with 41% of Americans choosing this screen for news, just above 37% for online.[40]

Yet there are consequences to the considerable time we spend with this medium. Several have been mentioned already such as the ability to transform perceptions of reality, cumulative effects, and narcotizing dysfunction, but because of the amount of time we spend with television, it is also our most pervasive persuader. So while the television experience is ongoing, so too is the persuasion.

Television was not always an ongoing experience. Early experiments resulted in the projection of simple stationary images but it was Philo T. Farnsworth's image dissector that was able to create and produce live images in 1927. Television underwent much refinement when it was introduced formally to the public at the 1939 World's Fair, held in New York City. The number of television sets in American homes was minimal but grew steadily by the 1950s. Programming in the early days was limited to only a few hours a day but still Americans gathered around the tiny black-and-white screen.

A color system introduced by CBS needed a special receiver, limiting the amount of viewers until RCA's system was introduced, which was compatible with the black-and-white sets already owned by the public. The first color network program aired in 1953 on the new system.

The television network system and programming were modeled after radio. Early network programming grew steadily and was produced and sponsored by the advertisers until the quiz show scandals of the 1950s ended the single-sponsor era of television. Television was drawing loyal audiences that had a dramatic impact on the exposure to the sponsor and their products. Show sponsors began to manipulate contestants and the questions asked on several different quiz shows in an attempt to build drama and viewership. The most famous of these scandals occurred in 1956 when it was revealed that *$64, 000 Question* winner Charles VanDoren was fed the answers and his opponent scripted to lose. A congressional hearing resulted in the end of single sponsored shows and the beginning of the spot commercial, which we still have today. The government was involved in this decision because the stations are issued licenses to operate in the public's interest; and their trust was violated.

The competition between networks increased with NBC and CBS, the forerunners to programming until the ABC caught up in the 1960s. The three held the largest share of the viewing audience through the 1980s. By the 1990s cable and newcomer Fox decreased their market share dramatically. Today NBC/Universal is owned by Comcast, ABC is owned by the Walt Disney Corporation, and in 2019 CBS merged with Viacom becoming ViacomCBS, though both companies fall under the control of National Amusements, and media conglomerate News Corp owns Fox.

These networks constitute broadcast television, television we can receive for free through a receiver, and their content is regulated via the Federal Communications Commission (FCC).

As with radio, television stations are issued licenses and frequencies, operate in the public's interest, and are subject to content regulations. Subscription-based television received via cable or satellite does not operate under the same regulations.

Broadcast television in particular relies on advertising for its primary source of revenue, while cable has both subscribers and advertisers as revenue streams. Both must target their audiences carefully to boost ratings and subsequently advertising. Advertisers look for networks and programming that aligns to the target audience they seek and places the ad accordingly—there is a reason why commercials for disposable diapers air during daytime television and not during major sporting events.

The sheer volume of television commercials has increased dramatically. A 30-minute television show is only 20–22 minutes of actual programming today. No other area of television advertising has grown as dramatically as infomercials. As a form of paid programming, the sponsor pays for the time slot to promote a product in an informative and entertaining manner.

The television-viewing audience has responded to the onslaught of commercials by "channel surfing" during commercials by using the commercial break on one channel to seek out other programming on another channel. Viewers often try to follow more than one show in a time slot using this method and annoying others in the room with them! Because we often record shows for later viewing, we also have a tendency to "zip" over the commercials to avoid viewing them when watching the playback. Some recorders will even eliminate commercials when recording.

Advertisers have had to respond to our methods of commercial avoidance by making commercials with a greater entertainment value resulting in what has been called "infotainment." The ads during the Super Bowl are a great example as many of these have a heightened entertainment value. Another method used by advertisers is called product placement where advertisers have their products placed within films and programs as props. This subject will be discussed in greater depth later in the chapter.

Like all other forms of media, television has new competition. While basic broadcast television can be viewed for free with a digital antenna, many Americans are choosing to "cut the cable" and turning away from cable or satellite services to alternatives through streaming platforms, that also allow consumers the ability to view their favorite shows from almost anywhere and without commercial interruption.

THE INTERNET AND THE WORLD WIDE WEB

Just as no one owns the airways in which radio and television is broadcast–no one owns the Internet. However, unlike radio and television, it is not regulated by a government agency. The Internet has been determined by the Supreme Court to be the most democratic medium available to us because it is user driven.

The Internet is a network of interconnected computers. The World Wide Web is an information system, on the Internet, consisting of information packets connected via links. In essence, the Internet is the hardware and the World Wide Web is the software.

The Internet began as ARPAnet (Advanced Research Projects Agency), a text-only military research communication network in 1969. In 1983 the National Science Foundation took over creating a network linking government-funded civilian research as well.

The early World Wide Web was strictly text based and the creation of Tim Berners-Lee in 1989. He is credited with the development of the following three fundamental elements, which allow us to connect and communicate worldwide:

1. hypertext markup language (HTML), which codes, stores, and retrieves messages;
2. universal resource locators (URL), which are essentially addresses assigned to every page on the Web;
3. hypertext transfer protocol (HTTP), which allows linked computers to communicate.

Berners-Lee also created the first Web browser. A Web browser is software that allows users to search files. Graphic interfaces followed, which allowed pictures and text in the same online document. This system allows us to click on an icon, thereby activating code to link to a source. We use this interface on our home computers as we double-click to open folders and activate pull-down menus that take us to other functions.

The Web is a form of nonlinear communication made possible through hypertext language. A user can choose what link to connect to, creating a user-driven medium where the user chooses what information to seek and in what sequence.

The Web permits us connectivity to an unlimited amount of information with a global reach. However, there is concern that children have few protections from the sometimes mature content found online. For instance, pornography is protected under the First Amendment, yet it can be easy for a child to stumble upon sites that contain pornographic material. For this reason, the Communications Decency Act was proposed in 1996. The Act called for the censorship or elimination of pornography from the Web. The Supreme Court deemed the Act unconstitutional citing again that the Web was the most democratic medium, as anyone can inexpensively post a site, and because it is user driven, we determine what sites we connect to. However, issues continue to plague the medium such as censorship, privacy rights, copyright, and access to information.

Censorship has been an ongoing concern with various groups calling for the suppression of some content on the Web, in particular extremist content, hate speech, and misinformation. For several years,

global entities have proposed holding social media sites like Facebook and Twitter be held responsible for content that is deemed harmful or misleading. They are not, because they only host the content that is posted by their users; and while the companies themselves are free from any litigation, that might come from controversial content, the users are not.

The openness of the Web and the ability to gather information about individuals has people concerned about privacy rights and protocols. The availability and ease of copying and downloading intellectual property is an issue for various industries and corporations. The Digital Millennium Copyright Act of 1998 stipulates that material on the Internet is protected intellectual property and that any copyright infringement or means to circumvent protections on intellectual property is a criminal act. Certainly the Recording Industry Association of America has made much of the illegal downloading of music files.

Proponents of universal access point out that the creators of the Web promoted free access, didn't receive compensation for their work, and were willing to place the technology in public domain, in other words it was free. Yet despite the fact that no one owns the Internet, we must pay Internet service providers (ISPs) to connect to it and because most of the ISPs are controlled by large corporations they then control accessibility. The counterpoint to this argument is that this is a service much like a utility service to which you pay a provider for your gas and electric. Just like those utilities there is an infrastructure that must be built to provide Internet service. But as more traffic is created online ISPs have capitalized on the ability to speed up traffic for some, while slowing down speeds or even blocking others. The idea of tiered services is appealing to the ISPs as a way to further generate revenue, as well as for companies that want to ensure that their content loads quickly and are willing to pay a premium to do so. However, smaller companies may not have the means to compete and even the average consumer can experience the throttling of connection speeds. As a result, Net Neutrality was proposed as a regulation in 2002, prohibiting an ISP from practicing data discrimination, and to ensure that data connections would be treated equally. The rules were approved in 2015 under President Obama, and repealed in 2018 under President Trump.

There are also cultural and social effects from this medium. We have become an information-based economy with the Web becoming the primary means of creating and distributing information including online forms, reference materials, and database information. This creates an access gap known as the "digital divide." While close to 75% of U.S. homes have Internet, Americans with lower incomes may not be able to afford computers or Internet connections, creating both an access gap and a knowledge gap.[41] Homes with a higher level of income and education tend to have greater access and therefore a greater knowledge potential. The gap is also generational as fewer elderly Americans have the level of connectivity as others.

Advertising has certainly become a revenue feature of many websites with banner ads, animated images, and pop-ups. Other characteristics of the Internet are that it can be anonymous, it has a global reach, it can be updated instantaneously, and it has an infinite capacity.

Compared to the other forms of media, the Internet is in its infancy, continually evolving and trying to gain control of itself. It is also unstructured and unregulated. Despite the issues that need to be addressed, the influence upon our society, and on other media, are immense.

New Media and Media Convergence

As media leave their traditional boundaries, and newer forms of media enter our lives, we not only adjust to the new forms but wonder how we lived without them, thus giving them power and the ability to influence us. Our ability to access media has increased dramatically as we can now stay connected through cell phones, tablets and even our watches. We download music, podcasts, movies, and television shows to our devices allowing us endless portability to even the more traditional media.

Where once students were resigned to spend endless hours researching in the stacks of the library where rows of bound print journals were

stored, today we can access a global abundance of information from the comforts of our homes, any hour of the day or late into the night.

There are podcasts for a variety of subjects and interests. College classes are offered online, if you need help writing a paper or citing sources help is a click away, at the Online Writing Lab through Purdue University, [42] and if you struggle with grammar, help is a podcast away with Grammar Girl.[43]

While there are numerous commercial and personal web sites that support the diversity of the Web, perhaps there are no better examples than the ability to express ourselves on social media where anyone, and everyone, can post videos, pictures, and messages for the world to see and share.

Perhaps the greatest influence is through media convergence where multiple media entities come together to form a hybrid of the two. Today there are online versions of newspapers and magazines, we can watch television shows that we might have missed online, and we can download playlists to our phone. Digital books can be downloaded and our cell phones capture photos and videos that can be uploaded to social media sites, and we keep digital diaries through online blogs.

⦿ ADVERTISING PERMEATES ALL MEDIA

The constant throughout most forms of media is advertising. It is advertising that is a major source of revenue for media and determines the number of pages in a newspaper or magazine, what programs will air and how they will be aired. Advertising is how American media is paid for.

Advertising can be as blatant as an infomercial or as subtle as product placement. Product placement occurs when companies pay to have their goods placed as props within film and television. This allows the film or television show to gain realism while the manufacturer gains increased exposure for their products. After E.T. munched on Reese's Pieces, sales soared; episodes of *The Apprentice* feature different companies and products in each weekly challenge; Starbuck's coffee was prominently featured in *Austin Powers: International Man of Mystery*; and in the James Bond film *Die Another Day* Ford introduced their latest version of the Thunderbird and 20 other companies paid a collective $70 million to have their products placed in that film.

⦿ CONCEPT CHECKLIST

media theories	concentration of ownership
deregulation	conglomerate
cross-media ownership	oligopoly
vertical integration	synergy
agenda setting	production
distribution	exhibition
network	affiliate
bias	omission
stereotypes	muckraking
broadcast television	cable television
radio format	formula programming

general interest magazine	advertorial
halftone	special interest magazine
national daily	metro daily
infotainment	infomercial
storyboard	establishing shot
transitions	shot
scene	sequence
cut	fade
dissolve	superimposition
wipe	zoom
tilt	dolly or tracking shot
pan	crane shot
product placement	editing
spot commercials	channel surfing
Internet	World Wide Web
Web browser	graphic interface
digital book	Internet service provider
blog	Telecommunications Act of 1996
media convergence	Digital Millennium Copyright Act
podcast	Federal Communications Commission

● SUMMARY

- There are several communication theories, such as uses and gratification, dependency, and cultivation, that illustrate the influence the media has on our perceptions, attitudes, and values.

- Media companies pressured for deregulation beginning in the 1980s.

- The Telecommunication Act of 1996 deregulated media, permitting companies to expand beyond their specific form, and into others as well.

- Companies that own several forms of media, or media-related businesses, are said to have achieved cross-media ownership.

- A company is vertically integrated when they have control over the media product from production through distribution to the consumer.

- The ability for a company to combine their various efforts is called synergy. Using the multiple companies that a conglomerate owns within various media industries to promote media products is a key advantage to cross-media ownership.

- Many major media conglomerates have global operations.

- Media companies are in business to profit.

- Agenda setting is the ability of the media to tell us what issues to think about, but not necessarily what to think about them.

- Many successful films, television shows, and even pop bands are copied to create other successful entities. Sometimes the formula is used multiple times creating spin-off series, sequels, and radio programming.

- The disparity between media portrayals and what most people consider to be beautiful is distorted The media and fashion industries are not reflecting the average man or woman in our society.

- Because media tends to use generalizations, there is a tendency toward bias and stereotypes.

- Daily newspapers can be published for a national or metro area.

- The *Wall Street Journal* and *USA Today* are national dailies with large circulations.

- Magazines can be classified as general interest or special interest.

- Radio was the first form of media to be regulated by a federal agency.

- The first network of interconnected radio stations became known as the National Broadcasting Company (NBC), followed by a second NBC-owned network, The Columbia Broadcasting System (CBS), and the Mutual Broadcasting System. NBC was forced to sell one network, which then became the American Broadcasting Company (ABC).

- The networks developed affiliate relationships with other stations to deliver network programming to larger audiences.

- Today radio is victim to formulaic programming and the concentration of ownership.

- The film industry has experienced a rich history of different eras characterized by advances in technology.

- There are several creative techniques used in motion pictures and television that are similar to photography.

- The television experience is intimate and ongoing.

- Broadcast television can be received for free through a receiver and the content is regulated via the Federal Communications Commission (FCC). Subscription-based television received via cable or satellite does not operate under the same regulations.

- Like radio and television, no one owns the Internet. However, radio and TV are reulated and the Internet is not.

- The Internet is a network of interconnected computers. The World Wide Web is an information system, on the Internet, consisting of information packets connected via links.

- The integration of technology and traditional media forms, such as online editions of newspapers, are examples of media convergence.

- Advertising permeates all forms of media and media depends on advertising for revenue.

⦿ **ACTIVITIES**

1. Select a section from the local newspaper. What kind of articles and information is in that section? Who is the target audience? What ads are in that section? What is the percentage of ads compared to the editorial content? How do the ads relate to the target audience? Is the placement strategic?

2. Watch a television show or film. How did they arrange the story line? In the introductory act, how were the characters and their situation introduced? In the second act, how did events unfold? What was the conflict? What obstacles were overcome? How was the situation resolved in the final act?

3. Discuss the various subjects and themes in today's media. How much of what is produced by the media is actually a reflection of what is occurring in our society? How much do you think these media themes influence our society? Does society reflect what they have consumed from media?

4. The American Film Institute has compiled a list of the 100 greatest American films of all time. How many have you seen? Try to check more off your list by watching a new film each month. Not sure why it was the chosen as the greatest? Look it up it might have been for an innovative theme or technique for the time. Check out the list on their site: https://www.afi.com/afis-100-years-100-movies-10th-anniversary-edition/

5. There are several different websites that list the seven different plots that are typically used in the film industry. See if you can use the list to categorize films that you watch.

6. Record one-hour segments of different television shows on cable or broadcast networks. Choose different times of the viewing day and different types of programming—daytime, primetime, sports, children's, etc. How many commercials run in that hour? Who are they targeted to? How do they relate to the audience?

7. Google yourself. Are you listed in the search? Why? What did you do that the search engine picked up on? Are you surprised by

the information? Are you concerned that it is listed? Do you have a googlegänger? A googlegänger is the digital version of a doppelgänger (a doppelgänger is someone's double). Is there someone else with your name? Why are they listed in the Web? Where are they from? Could you be confused with this person? Would you want to be?

● REFERENCES

Media Awareness Network
http://www.media-awareness.ca/english/issues/stereotyping/

Canadian media education site with valuable information on various media issues including stereotyping

A complete history of newspapers
http://encarta.msn.com/encyclopedia_761564853/Newspaper.html

Magazine Guide and Handbook 2008/09
http://www.magazine.org/content/Files/MPAHandbook0809.pdf

Detailed information on the scope of magazines

Columbia Journalism Review>Resources
http://www.cjr.org/resources/

An extensive list of major media companies with a detailed information on company holdings

Society of Professional Journalists
http://www.spj.org/ethics.asp

Code of Journalistic ethics

● ENDNOTES

1. Jay G. Bluhmer and Elihu Katz, "The Uses of Mass Communications: Current Perspectives on Gratifications Research," *Sage Annual Reviews of Communication Research Volume III*. (Beverly Hills, CA: Sage Publications, Inc.).

2. S. J. Ball-Rokeach and M. L. DeFleur (1976). "A Dependency Model or Mass-Media Effects," *Communication Research*, 3 (1976).

3. G. Gerbner, L. Gross, M. Morgan, and N. Signorielli, "Living with television: The dynamics of the cultivation process. In J. Bryant and D. Zillman (eds), *Perspectives on Media Effects* (pp. 17–40), (Hilldale, NJ: Lawrence Erlbaum Associates, 1986).

4. "Our Stations." iHeartMedia, 2020, www.iheartmedia.com/stations.

5. "What We Do." Federal Communications Commission, 10 July 2017, www.fcc.gov/about-fcc/what-we-do.

6. "Telecommunication Act of 1996," Federal Communications Commission, 10 July 2017, https://www.fcc.gov/general/telecommunications-act-1996

7. "FCC Broadcast Ownership Rules," Federal Communications Commission, 10 July 2017, https://www.fcc.gov/consumers/guides/fccs-review-broadcast-ownership-rules

8. Ibid.

9. "Sinclair's Defense Is as Bogus as the Shell Companies It Uses to Evade the FCC Rules." Free Press, 24 Oct. 2013, www.freepress.net/news/press-releases/sinclairs-defense-bogus-shell-companies-it-uses-evade-fcc-rules.

10. "SPJ Code of Ethics - Society of Professional Journalists." Society of Professional Journalists - Improving and Protecting Journalism since 1909, 6 Sept. 2014, www.spj.org/ethicscode.asp.

11. "Disney - Leadership, History, Corporate Social Responsibility." The Walt Disney Company, 2020, thewaltdisneycompany.com/about/#our-businesses..

12. "Our Businesses: News Corp." News Corp Our Businesses Comments, 2020, newscorp.com/about/our-businesses/.

13. Flood, Brian. "Fox Corporation Becomes Stand-Alone Company as Disney Deal Set to Close." Fox News, FOX News Network, 19 Mar. 2019, www.foxnews.com/entertainment/fox-corporation-becomes-stand-alone-company-as-disney-deal-set-to-close.

14. "Brands." Gannett, 2020, www.gannett.com/brands/.

15. Crossman, Ashley. "The Sociology of Social Inequality." ThoughtCo, Dashdot, 28 Jan. 2020, www.thoughtco.com/sociology-of-social-inequality-3026287.L. B. Lacey, "What Size is the "Average" Woman?", Full and Fabulous Website, <http://www.fullandfabulous.org/articles_view.asp?articleid=17064>

16. Levi Taylor, Jonah. "Height, Age, and Measurement Requirements of Modeling." How to Become a Model by Fitness Model Jonah Taylor,modelingwisdom.com/height-age-and-measurement-requirements-of-modeling.

17. "FastStats - Body Measurements." Centers for Disease Control and Prevention, Centers for Disease Control and Prevention, 3 May 2017, www.cdc.gov/nchs/fastats/body-measurements.htm.

18. Ibid.

19. "Products - Data Briefs - Number 360 - February 2020." Centers for Disease Control and Prevention, Centers for Disease Control and Prevention, 27 Feb. 2020, www.cdc.gov/nchs/products/databriefs/db360.htm.

20. Felsenthal, Julia. "Why Clothing Sizes Make No Sense." Slate Magazine, Slate, 25 Jan. 2012, slate.com/culture/2012/01/clothing-sizes-getting-bigger-why-our-sizing-system-makes-no-sense.html.

21. Ibid.

22. Goldman, Alison. "What Men Think About Women's Bodies." Glamour, Glamour, 13 Jan. 2016, www.glamour.com/gallery/what-men-think-about-womens-bodies.

23. Goldstein, Sasha. "Barbie as a Real Woman Is Anatomical-

ly Impossible and Would Have to Walk on All Fours, Chart Shows ." Nydailynews.com, 15 Apr. 2013, www.nydaily-news.com/life-style/health/barbie-real-womaan-anatomically-im-possible-article-1.1316533.

24.   Tough Guise, Jackson Katz, Media Education Foundation, 2000.

25. Vitelli, Romeo. "Media Exposure and the 'Perfect' Body." Psychology Today, Sussex Publishers, 18 Nov. 2013, www.psychol-ogytoday.com/us/blog/media-spotlight/201311/media-exposure-and-the-perfect-body.

26.   "Project #ShowUs." Dove US, www.dove.com/us/en/stories/cam-paigns/showus.html# and "Dove Self-Esteem Project." Dove US, www.dove.com/us/en/dove-self-esteem-project.html.

27. Bhardwaj, Prachi. "Advertisers Still Spend Almost as Much Money on Print Ads as PC Web Ads - Even Though Consumers Spend Far More Time Surfing the Net than Reading Newspapers." Business Insider, Business Insider, 15 May 2018, www.businessinsider.com/advertisers-spending-equally-print-desk-top-ads-charts-2018-5.

28. MPA Factbook, 2020, www.magazine.org/MPA/Research/MPA_Factbook/Magazine/Research_Pages/MPA_Factbook.aspx?h-key=1d597851-dd8b-455a-9dcf-4caad7688ff2.

29. Yu, Roger. "TEGNA, Gannett Go Separate Ways as Print Spin off Is Completed." USA Today, Gannett Satellite Information Network, 29 June 2015, www.usatoday.com/story/mon-ey/2015/06/29/tegna-gannett-split-completed/29455687/.

30.   Fischer, Sara. "Gannett and GateHouse's Parent Announced a Merger, and It Could Be a Way to Slow the Inevitable Decline of Local Newspapers." Business Insider, Business Insider, 6 Aug. 2019, www.businessinsider.com/gannett-and-gatehouse-an-nounce-merger-could-slow-newspaper-decline-2019-8.

31. "Our Mission." The Saturday Evening Post, 2020, www.saturda-yeveningpost.com/mission/.

32. Edward Bok, *The Americanization of Edward Bok*, "Cleaning Up the Patent Medicine and Other Evils < http://www.bartleby.com/197/30.html>

33. MPA Factbook, 2020, www.magazine.org/MPA/Research/MPA_Factbook/Magazine/Research_Pages/MPA_Factbook.aspx?h-key=1d597851-dd8b-455a-9dcf-4caad7688ff2.

34. Ibid.

35. Ibid.

36. "Time Flies: U.S. Adults Now Spend Nearly Half a Day Interacting with Media." Nielsen, 31 July 2018, www.nielsen.com/us/en/insights/article/2018/time-flies-us-adults-now-spend-nearly-half-a-day-interacting-with-media/.

37. "IHeartMedia Stations." IHeartMedia, 2020, www.iheartmedia.com/stations.

38. Geiger, A.W. "Key Findings about the Online News Landscape in America." Pew Research Center, Pew Research Center, 11 Sept. 2019, www.pewresearch.org/fact-tank/2019/09/11/key-findings-about-the-online-news-landscape-in-america/.

39. "Demographics of Internet and Home Broadband Usage in the United States." Pew Research Center: Internet, Science & Tech, Pew Research Center, 2019, www.pewresearch.org/internet/fact-sheet/internet-broadband/.

40. Purdue Writing Lab. "OWL // Purdue Writing Lab." Purdue Writing Lab, owl.purdue.edu/.

41. Girl, Grammar, and Books by Grammar Girl. "Grammar Girl." Quick and Dirty Tips, grammar.quickanddirtytips.com/EpisodeList.aspx>.

Chapter 8

The Component of
Message Processing

Chapter Objectives

- Identify various factors that factor in message processing.
- Explain how different people may perceive things differently from each other.
- Describe the central and peripheral routes of the Elaboration Likelihood Model.
- Explain how personality influences the interpretation of messages.
- Identify different Gestalt principles of perception.

Key Media Literacy Concept #5:
Different people experience the same message differently.

Key Media Literacy Question #5:
How might different people understand the message differently from me?

● ●

◉ MESSAGES ARE NOT INTERPRETED EQUALLY

The first three components of the Color Wheel Model discussed how messages are created to attract the attention of the audience and use different approaches to appeal to them. This component will look at how we interpret those messages and because we all bring different experiences to the interpretation process how interpretations may vary. Much of the interpretive process is based on various psychological factors and past experiences.

While messages are created for large audiences, and the primary goal is to have the general audience interpret the message equally, interpretation is still an individual process. We have all probably experienced differences in interpretation, you didn't get the joke that everyone else thought was hysterical or understand the point of a film or an ad campaign. However, once a message captures the attention of the audience, the interpretive process begins using different processing skills that have been developed with experience.

We already know that a message should be aligned to a specific target audience. The more that is known about that audience, the better that message can be specifically tailored to them. It is imperative to create that message to the interpretive abilities of the audience by understanding the depths of their acquired knowledge, their values and beliefs, what motivations they have, and even factoring in personality type.

⊙ PROCESSING MESSAGES

Cognitive processing is the ability to organize and evaluate information, and to problem-solve based on knowledge and understanding acquired through experience. We develop strategies to understand phenomena that are new to us or do not meet our expectations. The image in the Trojan ad of the pigs in a bar is not a normal occurrence and as such posed an interpretive problem for us to solve. It is a skill that develops with age as our experiences increase, and we add more to our memory.

Messages are processed through a variety of evaluative processes as we make judgments about the content of the message, evaluate its sender, and assess the value of the message to us.

Interpreting messages is similar to putting a puzzle together. We assess the elements within the message and determine how they fit together.

CONTENT ANALYSIS

One might assess the validity and logic of a message by looking for a rational claim with justifiable information. Statistical facts that can back up a claim can persuade us that an issue is of primary importance or convince us to buy a product.

Testimony and demonstrations lend credibility to messages. Statements from actual users of products are generally more believable than that of paid celebrities and demonstrations of products allow us to assess their capabilities for ourselves. News footage of unsafe water conditions at a nearby beach will probably keep even the most avid swimmer away until the situation is resolved.

Messages that reveal consequences of actions, issues, and events reveal the relation between cause and effect. For instance, if flooding in the Midwest and hail storms in the Northeast may have damaged much of the produce and crops for consumption by the American public, the likely consequences are rising prices and shorter supplies.

Messages can also develop credibility through the use of comparison. If a newspaper article reveals that a local intersection has had more traffic fatalities than any other, it is likely that local residents will use it as a call to action requesting changes through the highway authority.

VALUE-DRIVEN APPROACHES

Messages are also assessed for their value, such as the worth or usefulness of a product or the significance of an issue. In assessing the value of a message, one can determine whether it aligns with their behavioral patterns. Avid shoppers are more likely to rush to the latest end-of-season sale than the careful, regimented consumer. People who seek variety and excitement are more likely to travel, try new restaurants, and purchase the latest fashions. Others may value practicality, their home and family, and buy the basics. [1]

Problem solving and practicality are other value-driven approaches to message interpretation. The more we have a use for a product that we see in an ad or that it solves a difficult situation, the more likely we are to buy it.

The trustworthiness of a message source is also evaluated to determine if the message itself is credible. A message from an unknown or unreliable source is less likely to be believed.

⦿ INTERPRETATION AND PERSUASION

The Elaboration Likelihood Model developed by Richard Petty and John Cacioppo suggests that we process persuasive messages in different ways, at different times, and for different reasons based on motivation.[2] Let's say that you saw a commercial for a new restaurant opening in a nearby town. You didn't think much of it at the time because you don't travel that way often. But since then a friend invited you to join her for dinner and suggested that very restaurant. When you saw that same ad again, you paid closer attention because your motivation had changed.

The Elaboration Likelihood Model (ELM) proposes that we examine persuasive messages on a motivational continuum. On the low end is the peripheral route and on the high end the central route. In the example above the first evaluation of the restaurant ad used an approach close to the peripheral route, but as interest changed the analysis shifted using a process near the central route on the continuum.

Motivation is a key factor in message interpretation and we have already discussed how messages can be created to trigger various influences. While a message may serve to satisfy basic needs or fulfill higher level demands, much depends on the relevance of the message to us at that time such as the level of personal interest in the topic, the importance of the topic, and even our own temperament.

Ability is also a factor in the interpretation of messages. In the chapters relating to message creation, we discussed the need to understand the interpretive abilities of the audience. Much of this is based on accumulated knowledge and experience.

The central route involves high motivation and high involvement and therefore a great deal of elaboration. If, for instance, an article in the campus newspaper suggests that scholarship money was available for the asking, you would probably be motivated to learn the details. On the other hand, an article on the addition of a new brand of bottled water in the vending machines probably wouldn't make you rush to try it.

When analyzing a message using the central route, critical thinking skills are employed to evaluate the message characteristics. The source credibility is assessed, the ideas presented are scrutinized, and the merit of the message is evaluated for its value and the rationale behind it. A judgment is then made, and it is then that a strong argument can create a shift in attitude or cause persuasion to occur.

Because greater elaboration and a higher level of involvement has occurred in processing the message, the attitude shift or persuasion is likely to be significant. However, the reverse can occur as well. If after analyzing the message we find flaws or a lack of credibility, we are less likely to be swayed, so that critical thinking through the central route is also a deterrent to persuasion.

When evaluating a message on the lower end of the continuum, judgments are made much faster and with far less elaboration. The tendency is to evaluate based on situational characteristics such as source credibility and the benefits to one's self. There is no critical thinking as this is the path of least effort, with little audience motivation or indifference to the topic. It may be a situation where you know and like the source and like the idea. However, because there is no critical thinking, there is little resistance to persuasive messages particularly as they are absorbed through repetition.

It is imperative to realize that message interpretation does not occur on these two individual paths but along a continuum and that we slide along this continuum when processing messages depending on our need and interest at the time.

◉ THE INFLUENCE OF PERSONALITY TYPE

Personality characteristics are also factors in message processing. Some people are analytical by nature and enjoy the interaction of high-level critical thinking.[3] Personality type is a major influence to the interpretation of media messages.

Psychologists from Sigmund Freud to Carl Jung recognized that humans are creatures of habit and that there are not only patterns to our behavior but that we have preferential behaviors that we rely on. We are, in short, predictable. These personality traits even influence the manner in which we interpret media messages. To understand how we use these behavioral patterns, we must first identify them.

In 1921 psychologist Carl Jung identified several different functional types that have influenced countless assessment tools revealing personality preferences. The best known of these tests is the Myers-Briggs Type Indicator (MBTI), created in 1943 by the mother and daughter team of Katharine Cook Briggs and Isabel Briggs Myers.[4] This assessment tool has been used by colleges and universities to aid students in career counseling, by corporations to develop teamwork and leadership dynamics, and other means of personal and professional development. The indicator is significant to understanding message processing as it can help determine how we collect and interpret information and make decisions.

The Myers-Briggs Type Indicator is designed with opposing preferences in four function areas. Because we rely on favorite functions, a dominant function is determined in each of the four areas and when combined form one of the sixteen possible personality types.

The first pairing is Extraversion (E) or Introversion (I). Preferences in this area indicate where a person focuses their attention. People who are dominant in Extraversion are sociable, action oriented, and need to experience the world, while the those who prefer the traits of Introversion are more private, reflective, and need to understand the world.

The next set is a perceiving function. Preferences include Intuitive (N) or Sensing (S) and describe how a person acquires information. Intuitives rely on hunches and possibilities and are more theoretical. Sensors rely on their senses, are more reality based, and prefer detailed information.

Thinking (T) or Feeling (F) are a set of judging functions and describe how decisions are made. People with a dominance in Thinking prefer a rational logic system and are principled and analytical. Those with preferences in Feeling prefer a subjective value system to maintain harmony.

The last set is Judging (J) or Perception (P) and describes one's orientation to the outside world and their knowledge acquisition. People with a preference for Judging are structured, goal oriented, stable, and disciplined, while those that prefer Perception are process oriented, flexible and spontaneous, and disorganized procrastinators.

Once dominance is indicated in each of these functional areas, the combination determines the personality type. For instance, someone with dominant preferences in Extraversion (E), Sensing (S), Thinking (T), and Judging (J) is an ESTJ. Another individual may indicate preferences in Introversion (I), Intuitive (N), Thinking (T), and Perception (P) is an INTP. All sixteen possible personality types have distinct personality descriptions, and, as explained earlier, can help direct career and professional decisions as well as personal affairs.

Because the MBTI defines how one acquires and uses information, it is a valuable indicator that can help us understand how messages can be processed differently by different people. If a message appeals to certain personality types, it will be easier for that group to interpret, have a greater appeal, and be much more effective with the potential of affecting a greater audience response.

In fact, we can use this information to evaluate message processing in a growing trend in magazine advertising. Previously mentioned in Chapter 5, this trend is the creation of a magazine ad that relies on the extensive use of imagery with little or no supporting ad copy. We are left to our own interpretative abilities to process the ad's message based on the imagery. This trend started in higher-end magazines with a target

Registered mark of Pinacle Food Group LLC, used with permission

audience with higher incomes and levels of education because they had the cognitive abilities to interpret these messages. The trend has been trickling down to more mainstream publications over the years as we have become an increasingly visual society and have therefore become more visually literate.

The example pictured here is one of a series that Duncan Hines ran, featuring various women with different cakes and baked goods, where the top of their head should be. There is no ad copy only the tag line, "Create Your Own." The unusual imagery certainly helps the ad stand out from all of the rest, but what does it mean? The answer can be as varied as the number of people who are questioned. Some see the baked goods as a reflection of the person pictured in the ad. Here the chocolate shavings on the cake resemble the model's hair. Others suggest that the ads demonstrate the unique creations that can be accomplished with a boxed cake mix. Who is right? They all are because not only is beauty in the eye of the beholder but perception is as well.

The set of perceiving functions in the MBTI with preferences for Intuitive (N) or Sensing (S) are of particular interest for processing these messages because they describe how a person acquires information. Intuitives should find these types of ads more appealing as they prefer a more creative and abstract approach. Because Sensors like reality-based imagery, especially photographs, and factual information, they may find this approach less appealing.

Courtesy Natchez Collection from Henredon

PERSONALITY PREFERENCES
OF MESSAGE PROCESSING

SENSORS prefer:
- *a practical approach*
- *reality-based imagery*
- *to concentrate on details*
- *a utilitarian style*
- *factual information*
- *to identify benefits*
- *more text*

INTUITIVES prefer:
- *an abstract approach*
- *conceptual imagery*
- *implied aspects*
- *an imaginative style*
- *to speculate, assume information*
- *to envision possibilities*
- *more imagery*

The examples above help to illustrate this point. The Henredon ad is filled with imagery of an ornate bed and close-ups of the detailed craftsmanship but is without textual information. The Monroe Manor ad mockup, on the other hand, is complete with an image that includes not only the bed, but the optional pieces in the collection, as well as the name of the collection, pricing information, and sale dates. The ad is a complete package with little left to the reader, an appeal completely suited to the Sensor. Intuitives will fill in the information not supplied; imagining the possibilities for themselves while the Sensors prefer to have all the information supplied.

everything you need...   ...more of what you want

leather seats, premium Monroe Max sound system
with 12 speakers and 800 watts of power, back-up camera,
lane assistant package, blind spot monitor,
Ground Grabber traction system, optional winter package
offers heated seats and steering wheel, optional V6 engine,
bluetooth connection, available sunroof, premium tires,
and over 75 other safety features

test drive one at your
local dealer today

Some ads are designed as "crossover" ads, like the example ad above. The striking image suits the Intuitive who can see the roomy interior, leather seats, and a feature-filled console and dash. While the Sensor takes in this image as well, they benefit from the detailed ad copy that fills them in on all the features of the vehicle, seen and unseen.

Much can be said of the influence of personality as the dominant preferences create patterns to both our behavior and interpretive practices, yet this is not the only pattern-seeking approach to message processing.

● GESTALT PRINCIPLES OF PERCEPTION

Max Wertheimer, Wolfgang Köhler, and Kurt Koffka were among the German psychologists who applied Gestalt psychology to visual perception in the 1920s. Their ideas were radically different from the "atomistic" approach of the time. The atomistic theory approached interpretation through the evaluation of separate elements, disregarding the context.

As we know, visual information is a collection of elements. Gestalt theorists believe that we process information not just through the individual elements in a piece, but that the context or surrounding information is equally important. This perception aligns with information presented in Chapter 3; that meaning occurs within a context or setting, and if that environment or context changes, the meaning may shift. Therefore, as Gestalt

theory suggests, the whole is greater than the sum of its parts.

This point can be illustrated using the image of the painting above. When looking at the image, we might recognize it as a beautiful landscape because we are taking in the whole of its contents. Chances are less likely someone would walk away from it commenting only on the boat in the background.

Gestaltists also believe that visual perception is a process of organizing information by seeking visual patterns. There are a several Gestalt principles that describe these patterns.

FIGURE AND GROUND

The first of these patterns is figure and ground, where we seek to distinguish the primary elements from the background. In this image, it is easy to discern the figure of the tree from the background, but then there are secondary images in the negative space–the profiles of a gorilla and a female lion.

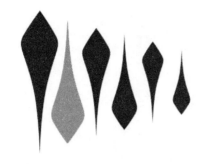

SIMILARITY

When elements look alike because of size, shape, or color, they tend to be perceived as a group. We see the darker shapes as similar and the one lighter shape as different from the others. But just as we notice similarity, we also recognize the dissimilarity of the circles within the rows of squares in the last example.

PROXIMITY

Elements that are close to each other are perceived as a group. Each square, with its embedded circle, becomes a separate group. The pairings are seen as perceived as a single unit because they are placed in close proximity to each other.

FAST LANE
GRAPHICS

CONTINUATION

Continuation occurs when the eye follows a continuous path that is real or perceived. In this example, the eye will generally start at the bottom of the highway image and follow the element upward. This same principle of Gestalt is why our eye travels around a circle to read the text in the second example,

CLOSURE

Because the mind prefers closed or stable shapes, it has the tendency to fill in missing information and close gaps. This is why we perceive the first example to be a circle rather than a series of individual dots. Although the second example consists of five books arranged in a circular fashion, our mind perceives the negative space as a star by closing off the open ends.

System to Access Resources (S.T.A.R.) logo for the Dallas Public Library. Design: Brett Baridon. By Permission.

EQUILIBRIUM

The mind seeks order as we prefer organization, balance, and simplicity. The symmetrical image of the trees, water and sky is balanced and we find comfort in the even distribution of weight.

Another aspect of equilibrium is the natural order of things. We know from experience that these are evergreen trees because of the natural and expected shape of them and that of the representation of the water.

ISOMORPHIC CORRESPONDENCE

This principle of Gestalt reiterates a major point of this book, that meaning is derived from our experiences and memories. We know from experience and memory recall what is likely to happen to the bubble created by the bubble gum as it increases in size.

⦿ CASE IN POINT
IDENTIFYING PRINCIPLES OF GESTALT

Design Firm: Harp and Company; Client: Joseph Ferratella; Designers: Douglas G. Harp, Linda E. Wagner and Scott McFarland

Analyzing the elements

As always first assess the denotative elements in the piece. There are letterforms that appear to spell out Ferratella's Lawn Grooming with the tops cut off some of the letterforms.

Searching for Gestalt principles

Focusing in on the cut-off letterforms, and looking back at our list of principles, our mind tries to piece these segments together. In doing so, we are closing the letterforms to make sense of this message. We can use closure because the segments are in close proximity to each of their counterparts.

We are able to discern these elements, or figures, from the background and read across a continuing line of text thereby using both figure and ground as well as continuation. The piece simulates the trimming of grass as the clippings fly from the passing of the lawn mower blade—something we can recall from our past experiences.

Summing it up

This piece uses several principles of Gestalt primarily, closure, proximity, figure and ground, continuation, and isomorphic correspondence and is an excellent example of how several principles can be used within a given piece.

● CONCEPT CHECKLIST

motivation

Myers-Briggs Type Indicator

Elaboration Likelihood Model

peripheral route

persuasion

personality influence

central route

gestalt

● SUMMARY

- Messages are processed based on an individual's values, attitudes, beliefs, and accumulated social knowledge.

- Messages are interpreted differently by different people.

- Persuasion may occur when a rational message from a credible source is aligned to the target audience.

- The Elaboration Likelihood Model (ELM) suggests that we process persuasive messages in different ways, at different times, and for different reasons based on motivational continuum.

- The two primary routes of the elaboration likelihood model used to process messages are the central and peripheral routes.

- The peripheral route is characterized by a low motivation factor and the central route by a high motivation factor including critical thinking skills.

- Personality type is also a factor in processing messages.

- The Myers-Briggs Type Indicator is an assessment tool used to that reveal personality preferences to how we collect and interpret information to make decisions.

- Sensor types prefer realistic imagery and factual information while intuitive types prefer abstract imagery with little or no information.

- We process messages based on the context in which it is presented.

- Gestaltists believe that to process imagery in messages we organize information by seeking visual patterns.

- There are several Gestalt principles that describe visual patterns.

⊙ RESOURCES

Online

Personality type quizzes and information
This is one of several free resources online to determine your personality type that use the Myers-Briggs Type Indicator as a basis. Along with the survey to identify your personality type, the site also contains additional information explaining the 16 different personality types as well as the best career choices for each type, their learning and leadership styles, and typical communication strategies.

http://www.humanmetrics.com/cgi-win/JTypes2.asp

Gestalt principles of perception
This is one of several sites that offer explanations and examples of the various Gestalt principles of perception. Just be sure to search for "Gestalt principles of perceptions" not just gestalt, as Gestalt is a far reaching study within the field of psychology.

https://www.usertesting.com/blog/gestalt-principles

⊙ ACTIVITIES

1. Find out what your personality type is. There are several online tests similar to the Myers-Briggs Type Indicator. Are you a Sensor or an Intuitive? Which kind of imagery do you prefer? Does it match the assessment in the chapter?

2. How can you use the personality information to help you with professional career choices or understanding relational issues?

3. Select a print ad and identify as many principles of Gestalt as you can.

4. Take that same ad and determine which personality type would be more attracted to the piece.

⦿ ENDNOTES

1. "VALS™: US VALS™ Survey: SBI." Strategic Business Insights, 2020, www.strategicbusinessinsights.com/vals/presurvey.shtml.

2. "Richard E. Petty, John T. Cacioppo, and David Schumann, "Central and Peripheral Routes to Advertising Effectiveness: The Moderating Role of Involvement," *Journal of Consumer Research*, 10, no. 2, (September, 1983).

3. Ibid.

4. The Myers & Briggs Foundation - MBTI® Basics, 2020, www.myersbriggs.org/my-mbti-personality-type/mbti-basics/.

5. P. LaBarbera, P. Weingard, and E. Yorkston, "Matching the Message to the Mind," *Journal of Advertising Research*, (Sep/Oct) 1998).

6. Ibid.

The Component of
Action

Chapter Objectives

- Identify different ways people respond to messages.

- Evaluate the methods in which groups react to media messages.

- Explain how the creators of media might use this information.

- Identify the various purposes of a media message.

Key Media Literacy Concept #6:
Media messages are created to influence an audience response.

Key Media Literacy Question #6:
Why was this message sent and how does it impact the audience?

. . . .

◉ MESSAGES GENERATE AN ACTION

The processing of a media message results in an interpretation. A judgment has been made based on motivation, values, abilities, and various personality factors, and leads to the final action, a response. This chapter, representing the last component of the Color Wheel Model, reflects the culmination of the long journey of a media message. This is the end result; the actions that the audience takes after processing those media messages. Those actions vary widely and can occur as individual actions or in a group.

◉ INFLUENCED TO ACT

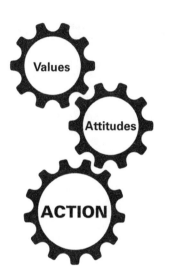

An influential media message will inspire us to respond in a variety of methods and for very diverse reasons but first we have to assess our level of awareness.

AWARENESS

Depending on how dependent we are on media and the forms of media we use the most, we may or may not be aware of issues, news stories, concerns, events, new music or movie releases, or any number of community, national, or global particulars. Greater awareness creates a greater library of acquired knowledge that can be applied in to any number of situations and can build a greater understanding of the world. This store of information also forms the basis for critical thinking when deciphering media messages. The level of awareness that an individual may have could be assessed through conversation with others, educational assignments, job interviews, and more everyday interactions.

Often traditional marketing research determines the level of awareness of an audience by identifying the familiarity of a message and its contents. Respondents may be asked how they came to be aware of a community issue, if they heard a specific radio spot, saw an ad for a particular product, or can even identify companies, organizations, and institutions. Usually they are also asked to supply as much information about the topic as they can to determine whether the message communicated effectively.

INFLUENTIAL CONTENT

Many resources are spent determining how and why we consume goods and services, including the media.

While it is important for an audience to be aware of a message and its informational content, it is equally important to determine the impression made on the audience. We can be influenced by both the message and the messenger but also need to be able to evaluate both.

Aside from our obsession with celebrities, as messengers they often create an enhanced sense of credibility, and their notoriety often leads to a false a sense of competence. It is for this reason that people find them trustworthy, accepting the products, events, causes, or political views they are promoting, and even electing them into office. We have to be aware that often these celebrity spokespersons are often paid for those messages.

The content of the message should also be impactful. Advertising strives for a balance of informational and entertainment value, while news outlets strive for messages that are informational and unbiased. All have an agenda, all have a corporate culture behind them.

Media effects theories have shown that over time, exposure to violent media content can cause several different reactions by society. Many are desensitized to it, to the point that we accept it as normal. And in some cases aggressive behavior is also normalized as the means to an end. For others, these messages signal a mean and frightening world with danger around every corner.

Rather than blind acceptance, our actions should center on evaluating both the message and the messenger. Critical thinking will reveal the implications or assumptions so that we can respond as well informed citizens.

CONSUMERISM

Another response to media messages is the increased acquisition of goods and services. The first spikes in the purchases of goods began when national ads started to run in the earliest forms of newspapers and magazines enticing the audience to buy new food products, cloth-

ing, and even kit homes where all of the components to build a house were pre-cut, labeled, bundled, and delivered to the building site with instructions. As media began to develop and become more pervasive, so to did the exposure to new products and ideas. Today we are inundated with messages from commercials on traditional media, to pop-up and banner ads online, or the ads that interfere with our apps.

Many strive to maintain their appearance in a manner that emulates what they see in the media whether that be the brands they wear, their style of hair, or their body image. Far too many of

There are a variety of ways for people to respond to media messages and as many different reasons why.

us spend beyond their means, lacking the ability to separate what they want from what they need. As a result, the national average for credit card debt, in households that have unpaid balances, is over $15,000 and is second only to students loan debt which averages far higher with an average of $29,000.[1]

An enormous amount of money is spent each year on market research to track responses to products, services, and even political candidates. There is an endless list of questions that can be asked of any audience such as their likes and dislikes of a product, their level of brand loyalty, who they will vote for, what streaming services they subscribe to, what college a high school senior has chosen to attend, and so on.

A knowledgeable consumer, armed with self-discipline and knowledge has the means to counteract the onslaught of persuasive messages instead of yielding to the increasing demands of a consumer society.

PSYCHOLOGICAL AND BEHAVIORAL RESPONSES

How we feel about someone or something, whether that be a product, politician, the content of a message, or a community issue, can motivate decision-making processes. What we value and believe in will often control our responses. Quite often our emotional responses can also fuel our behavior.

As we see natural disasters taking place in our world has prompted people to donate to fund raising campaigns or to participate in community clean-up events. A health care crisis like COVID-19, prompted people to participate in everything from nightly acknowledgments to healthcare workers, donations to food drives, support of local restaurants, and checking in on elderly neighbors. Human atrocities, like the brutality shown to people of color, prompted the Black Lives Matter movement along with political protests. Our values shift as a result of these situational concerns. We become more aware of issues, even if we are not directly affected, and we have an opportunity to hear from those that are. When we are open to listening to other viewpoints, and can accept the concerns and inequities that exist for some, then we have the first steps toward tolerance and acceptance, and then the means to challenge the status quo. Such is the case with the Black Lives Matters movement as greater numbers of people from all walks of life have joined in the protests calling for change.

Sometimes change is more subtle as our values shift. Societies ideas of heroes is a good example. Before the terrorists attacks of 9/11, professional athletes were the predominant hero figures, while after 9/11 first responders became the embodiment of a hero. The COVID-19 pandemic has shifted that representation to include healthcare workers.

Our emotions and concerns can lead to a response to calls for action that can have impactful results on our communities and legal systems.

⦿ GROUP RESPONSES TO MEDIA MESSAGES

While much of the previous information concentrated on the many different responses to media messages that an individual may have, untraditional research has revealed mass audience responses to media messages.

Mark Ritson, a British marketing professor, found a unique approach to gathering research information. By agreeing to teach media education classes in six London area schools, he was granted access to the most media-savvy demographic—the adolescent.[2] Through intensive observation and interviews, his findings revealed that this group responded to their exposure to media messages, and specifically advertising, in a highly social manner. The researcher's findings revealed that responses to media messages resulted in social interaction, and that several cultural themes were apparent.

Researchers have identified ways in which groups respond to media messages and adapt them to their lives.

Despite the fact that this research focused on a specific demographic in a limited area, the findings are quite observable across demographic groups elsewhere. We have all probably witnessed the following variants of the "social use" of media messages.[3]

GROUP DISCUSSION AND EVALUATION OF MEDIA TEXTS

Groups who come in contact with a media text have a tendency to discuss it as a group, particularly if they experienced the text together. Say, for example, a group of students from the dorm decide to go to a movie and grab a bite to eat afterward. The topic of conversation easily turns to the film as members of the group speak of their observations and reactions. The film becomes the means in which they are interacting socially. Often these discussions serve to aid in the interpretive process, as perceptions and various meanings are evaluated, resulting in a deeper level of understanding for the group.

Even if a text is experienced separately, for example a student waiting for class to start can bring it up in conversation, and those who experienced it as well can add to the discussion. These shared experiences can act to create a common bond. But those who did not have contact with the media text are unable to reciprocate. They are the "odd man out," unable to socialize on the same level as the others.

RITUALIZING AND APPLICATION OF MEDIA TEXTS

Media texts often reflect cultural values and create cultural meanings at the same time. Verbal and physical elements that are repeated in advertising, entertainment, and educational or informational media

are often absorbed, ritualized, and applied in new contexts. Scenes from a favorite movie may be reenacted, dialogue repeated or mimicked, and gestures assimilated. Air quotes, the hand-heart popularized by Taylor Swift, and the Vulcan salute, from Star Trek, are all examples of ritualized gestures, and when given an opportunity to be on a boat who hasn't stood at the bow with their arms outstretched like Jack and Rose in Titanic?

Catchphrases from songs, movies, television shows, and commercials find their way into our everyday conversations on a regular basis. "I'll be back" (Terminator), "Show me the money" (Jerry Maguire), "May the force be with you" (Star Wars), "Why so serious?" (The Dark Knight), and "May the odds be ever in your favor" (Hunger Games) have become regular interjections to our dialogue. Some catchphrases like "Whassup?" (Budweiser) achieved massive assimilation into the culture and language.

Advertising jingles and slogans from ad campaigns are often so memorable that we might find ourselves singing them because they are stuck in our heads, which, of course, is the point.

Media messages are often recycled by other forms of media. Parodies are a method of ritualizing media messages in an attempt to satirize or poke fun at the original. Memes are a good examples of humorous or satirical parodies.

Visual parodies include gestures like the double face slap made famous in the film Home Alone, which is actually an imitation of the famous painting The Scream by Edvard Munch.

While some rituals are timeless, for many their appeal often wanes until it is no longer "cool" to use them. Although people still utter "whassup" from time to time, it no longer has the impact it once did.

Parodies imitate other works. The gesture imitated in the movie Home Alone parodied the famous painting The Scream and this image mimics them both.

◉ A CYCLICAL PURPOSE

This last component is the culminating effect of message processing which requires a judgment based on one's attitudes, values, and ideologies.

While audiences may act individually there are also group responses where several individuals can fuel responses off each other.

Messages are created to inform, entertain, educate, and to persuade. The public should be mindful that these messages occur in a commercial environment, and as such have a commercial agenda. This should then be at the core of every decision that is made, every action that is taken. We need to be very conscious of the persuasion that can easily influence us to purchase goods and services too freely, or to react emotionally or behaviorally.

The cycle is then complete and set to begin again. Either the audience responds through symbolic action or with their own messaging or the messengers craft new media messages based on their responses.

⬤ CONCEPT CHECKLIST

messsage purpose	response	advocacy
consumerism	social use	ritualization
group evaluation	catchphrases	parody
emotional response	behavioral response	consumerism

⬤ SUMMARY

- Media messages have a purpose.

- Media messages are created to stimulate an audience to action.

- The response to messages is primarily an individual act.

- Responses are dependent on motivation, personal involvement, and situational contexts.

- There are many different means in which people may respond based on the purpose of the message, as someone may be persuaded to buy a product or information may prompt a call to action.

- Group responses include the discussion and evaluation of advertising, the ritualization of gestures or other behaviors, adapting media catchphrases into our everyday language, and the parody or mimicking of media messages.

- The response messages received may dictate how new messages are created.

⦿ ACTIVITIES

1. Make a list of catchphrases from films, television, and commercials that we have adapted into our everyday language. How many can you come up with? What about gestures that originated in the media?

2. Memes are essentially parodies or spoofs of other media messages. Identify the parody and assess what they are mimicking. How have they adjusted the meaning of the original message? What new message was created by the meme?

3. How many adaptations of the painting "American Gothic" by Grant Wood can you find?

4. What have you purchased recently that you didn't need but wanted? Have you ever bought something only to regret it later? What promted you to make the purchase?

5. Have you entered into a recent group discussion regarding a shared media event? Try this experiment. The next time you are with a group ask them if they have seen, read, or heard of a specific film, television show or the like. Choose something most of the group is likely to have seen and see where the conversation goes. Then choose something more obscure and see how the conversation changes. Are there some people who no longer participate in the conversation? How have the group dynamics changed?

6. Find out what kind of consumer you are. Take the Values, Attitudes and Lifestyles (VALS) survey at http://www.sric-bi.com/VALS/presurvey.shtml. The survey results will reveal your primary and secondary types. How accurately did the survey describe your consumer type? Discuss the impact of this type and/or other marketing research on the consumer and the economy

⦿ RESOURCES

Online

There are several online lists of the most memorable catchphrases from films, television shows and commercials. There are others that include advertising slogans and taglines.

This one lists the top 60 TV catchphrases is from TV Guide: https://www.tvguide.com/news/tvs-60-greatest-catchphrases-1070102/

Find out what kind of consumer you are. The tool on this website, a survey, categorizes consumers by types.

VALS marketing and consulting tool
http://www.strategicbusinessinsights.com/vals/presurvey.shtml

Articles

Ritson, M., and Elliott, R. (1999). "The Social Uses of Advertising: An Ethnographic Study of Adolescent Advertising Audiences." *Journal of Consumer Research*, 26.

⦿ ENDNOTES

1. Friedman, Zack. "Student Loan Debt Statistics In 2020: A Record $1.6 Trillion." Forbes, Forbes Magazine, 5 Feb. 2020, www.forbes.com/sites/zackfriedman/2020/02/03/student-loan-debt-statistics/

2. M. Ritson, and R. Elliott, "The Social Uses of Advertising: An Ethnographic Study of Adolescent Advertising Audiences," Journal of Consumer Research, 26 (1999).

3. Ibid.

4. Adbusters is an anti-consumer group that supports a magazine that is well known for their spoof ads. Many of these ads can be found at http://www.adbusters.org/gallery/spoof ads.

Part III

Appendix A
Glossary

Access—The means by which we identify and gain entry to the various forms of media.

Acquired knowledge—What we have come to understand, based on our past experiences and education.

Action—The component of the Color Wheel Model of Media Communication that examines the purpose of media message, and how those message elicit responses.

Affiliate—A local broadcaster, that carries some, or all, of the programming of a television or radio network, but is owned by someone other than the owner of the network.

Agenda setting—The attempt of the media to tell the public what issues should be of concern, which could be motivate out of genuine concern, or for their ratings.

Analysis—Examining the structure and contents of a media message.

Appeal strategies—Tactics used to create urges within an audience.

Aristotle—A philosopher and educator from ancient Greece, who studied under Plato and tutored Alexander the Great.

Arrangement—The means in which a message is organized.

Bias—Prejudice in favor, or against, someone or a group.

Blog—Website where a group of individuals are able to maintain digital diaries or journals.

Brand imperialism—A company that achieves global recognition, not only promotes their product but american culture onto other countries via their marketing eforts

Broadcast television—Television that we can receive for free through a receiver, and the content is regulated by the Federal Communications Commission.

Cable television—Subscription-based television, received via cable or satellite providers, and the content is not regulated by the FCC.

Camera angle—Determines the position of the photographer in relationship to the subject: front, side, above, and below.

Canons of rhetoric—The guiding principles to effective communication.

Catchphrases—A well-known sentence or phrase, like a slogan motto, jingle, or tag line, that becomes a regular part of our dialogue.

Central Route—Part of the Elaboration Likelihood Model, this route involves a person's high motivation and involvement.

Channel—The vehicle in which the message is sent or received.

Channel surfing—The tendency for a television viewer to sample multiple different channels during the same time frame.

Citizen journalism—Information that is gathered, shared, and analyzed by the average citizen usually through social media

Color Wheel Model of Media Communication—A theoretical illustration of a communication theory, with different sectors representing the different elements, or core concepts of media literacy.

Communication sphere—The sum of our experiences, accumulated social knowledge, values, attitudes, and beliefs that we bring with us to the communication process.

Composition—The artistic arrangement of various elements to produce a work.

Concentration of ownership – The trend in media ownership where a smaller number of corporations own larger number of media related companies.

Conglomerate—A large corporation formed by the merging of separate and diverse companies.

Connotation—The implied meaning of a message.

Consensual agreement—The shared social knowledge that allows us to communicate.

Construction—The component of the Color Wheel Model of Media Communication dealing deliberate choices in the creation of a message, with consideration of strategic signs and symbols, and connotative meanings in a specific context.

Consumer research—Conducting studies to find out the demographics of consumers in a market.

Context—Frame of reference, including background, environmental, and situational relationships.

Crane shot—A crane is used to film shots from overhead, the camera is positioned on a long, extendable, telescoping arm.

Creation—The production of messages.

Creative approaches—Techniques utilized within messages to entice an audience.

Creative Language—The component of the Color Wheel Model of Media Communication that deals with the application of creative approaches and appeals strategies to a message to make it enticing to the audience.

Critical thinking—Unbiased evaluation and analysis of issues, messages, and texts

Cross-media ownership—The ability of a corporation to own companies in various types of media industries.

Cut—A common transition joining two shots together, a simple break or cut in the film to the next shot.

Deconstruction—The act of analyzing a message.

Delivery—The means in which a message is conveyed, rendered, or distributed.

Denotation—The literal meaning of a message.

Deregulation—The lifting of restrictions and limitations on media ownership.

Digital book – A portable technology allowing a user to read books in a digital format.

Digital manipulation – Altering, or editing, of imagery through the use of computer hardware and software.

Digital Millennium Copyright Act—Passed in 1998, it said that material on the Internet is protected intellectual property, and any infringement is a criminal act.

Dissolve—The act of layering a fade-out and fade-in together, however, the screen never goes black, with the first image blurring into the second.

Distribution—The supplying or sharing of media products.

Dolly or tracking shot—Used to film subjects in motion, the camera is placed on a cart that moves along a track.

Editing—The choosing, or arranging of, material for a media product that creates a coherent storyline.

Elaboration Likelihood Model—A model that says we process persuasive messages in different ways, at different times, and for different reasons based on motivational continuum.

Elements of design—Basic components of design that constitute the compositional arrangement.

Emotional appeal—A common creative approach that taps into our feelings, sentiments, and instincts, to reach an audience.

Establishing shot—An opening shot that places the subject in the context of their surroundings or environment.

Ethos—One of Aristotle's three artistic proofs, moral competence, dealing with the credibility and character of the sender.

Evaluate—Making a judgment about the content of a media message.

Exhibition—The display of media products.

Fade—A common technique used to transition between scenes, either fading from black, or down to black. Often used to represent the passage of time, or to open and close a film.

Fake news—A form of misinformation that is biased, or designed to mislead or sensationalize, often to create harm against another. Claim usually made certain parties who feel that their perspective is not reported accurately, even when it may be.

Fallacy—An argument based on invalid reasoning.

Federal Communications Commission—U.S. Government entity regulates media communications by radio, television, satellite, and cable.

Feedback loop—Interaction between the sender and receiver, ensuring clarification with a greater possibility of successful communication.

Focal point—The point of emphasis, or the center of interest.

Formula programming—A method of reproducing a media product, based on the successful original.

General-interest magazine—A magazine with a broad range of topics, appealing to wide range of people.

Gestalt—Gestaltists believe that to process imagery in messages we organize information by seeking visual patterns.

Graphic interface—Allows pictures and text within the same online document.

Group evaluation—The informal ability of people, who when they are together evaluate forms of media messages.

Halftone—The technique of reproducing images in print, produced by dots of ink.

Humor—Appeal strategy designed to make a message amusing or light-hearted.

Image continuum—A continuous sequence of imagery beginning with the most realistic, moving through various stages of abstraction, to pure iconic symbol.

Infotainment—Broadcast material that is intended to entertain and inform.

Infomercial—A television commercial that promotes a product and is designed to look like a television program.

Internet—A network of interconnected computers.

Internet service provider—Company providing a connection for a consumer to access the Internet.

Invention—The reasoning and rationale behind an argument, or the means of justifying the main message of an argument.

Linear model—A theoretical illustration of a communication theory that is characterized by one-way communication.

Logos—One of Aristotle's three artistic proofs, outlining that an argument be based on logic and reason.

Maslow's Hierarchy of Needs—The identification of the five basic human needs, prioritized within a hierarchy.

Media consumption—The various ways in which we interact with, and experience, all forms of media sources, from watching television to buying media products, as well as the influence of media on our day-to-day purchases.

Media convergence—With new technologies, multiple media entities are able to come together and form a hybrid of the two.

Media literacy—An educational approach with the purpose of empowering people with the ability to use critical thinking skills when consuming media, thereby creating an awareness for the characteristics of media, the intent of its messages, the techniques used, and its impact on society.

Media Operations—The component of the Color Wheel Model of Media Communication that looks at the various forms of mass media, the media agenda, and the resulting limiting points of view.

Media regulation—Rules that manage and license media outlets for content, ownership, competition, and ethics.

Media theories—A series of propositions intended to describe, or explain, a media experience or occurrence.

Mediated culture—Culture that is shaped by the influence of our media.

Memory—The ability to recall, recognize, and remember information, emotions, and feelings.

Message—A verbal, written, visual, or recorded communication.

Message credibility—Communication that can be believed in or trusted due to a level of quality.

Message processing—The component of the Color Wheel Model of Media Communication that characterizes the psychological process of perception that examines how we accumulate and apply knowledge, reasoning through persuasion, and interpreting messages.

Metaphor—A figure of speech, or trope, that uses and unrelated object to represent another.

Metro daily—A newspaper published daily for a regional metropolitan market.

Motivation—A desire or willingness to process a message.

Muckraking—The investigative reporting that exposes societal issues.

Myers-Briggs Type Indicator—An assessment tool that defines personality types, based on Karl Jung's theories for psychological motivations and patterns for preference.

National daily—A newspaper published daily for a national audience.

Network—A group of broadcasting stations that simultaneously air the same programming, not necessarily owned by the same company.

Noise—Obstacles to exchanging information and communication.

Oligopoly—A state of limited competition, where the market has a small number of competing companies.

Omission—The action of excluding, or leaving something out.

Open mindset—The ability to be willing to rationally consider, and even accept, new ideas, arguments, and information. It is imperative to critical thinking.

Pan—The ability of the camera lens to move left or right.

Pathos—One of Aristotle's three artistic proofs, outlining the emotional appeal to an audience.

Perception—Forming an impression or understanding of a message based on our past experiences and knowledge. A perception does not mean this understanding is the intended interpretation.

Peripheral Route—Part of the Elaboration Likelihood Model, this route suggests low motivation and involvement.

Personality influence—The effect that personality type has on processing messages.

Persuasion—The ability of media messages to influence behaviors through reasoning of an argument or message.

Pictograph—A pictorial symbol representing a concept or object.

Podcast—Digital media files that are distributed over the Internet for playback on portable media players and computers.

Principles of design—The relational concepts that guide compositional design.

Produce—Create original independent messages.

Product placement—The prominent positioning of goods and products as props within film and television.

Production—The making, or manufacturing, of media products.

Radio format—The musical genre and programming style of a radio station.

Receiver – The decoder of the message.

Response—Obtaining feedback from customers regarding their experiences with a product.

Rhetoric—The artful use of verbal, nonverbal, visual, and written communication to have a persuasive effect.

Ritualization—The adoption of a custom, procedure, gesture, or saying, from media and the integration into everyday life.

Rule of thirds—The division of the viewfinder into horizontal and vertical thirds, and using the intersecting points to place the subject.

Scene—A series of shots, using the same characters, to build the action of a film.

Schema theory—The ability to use stored data, or accumulated knowledge, to interpret media messages.

Semiotics—The study of signs and symbols.

Sender—The creator or encoder of the message.

Sequence—A series of scenes connected by an event.

Sex appeal—A common appeal strategy using physical attraction to instill desire.

Shot—A series of frames of continuous film, without a break in that continuity.

Signs/symbols—A sign designates something to which meaning is attached. A symbol is an object used to represent something abstract like a concept.

Social media—Applications and websites used to communicate with others through social networking.

Social use—The role that media plays within the social context of our social interactions.

Special interest magazine—A magazine geared to a niche audience with a very narrow focus.

Spot commercials—A television advertising segment paid for by a single sponsor.

State owned media—Mass media that is supported financially and under editorial control of a country's government, either directly or indirectly.

Stereotypes—A generalized image, or idea, usually connected to a person, or group of people.

Storyboard—A sequence of drawings meant to visualize a script for film, television, or commercials.

Structure—The component of the Color Wheel Model of Media Communication that deals with the methodology, or framework, in which a message is constructed.

Style—The manner, or technique, that is used to give a message flair.

Stylistic devices (or tropes)—Creative media approaches that are derived from language, also known as tropes.

Subsidized media—Media that receives some form of benefit, such as funding, tax relief, or production, usually from the government.

Superimposition—A technique where two images appear together on screen, however, unlike a dissolve, the images remain together on screen.

Synergy—The ability for a company to combine efforts using the companies it owns within various media industries to promote and strengthen the company.

Target audience—The specific demographic for a medium or message.

Telecommunications Act of 1996—Legislation passed by Congress, updating a series of media regulations, including the loosening of laws with limitations on media ownership, paving the way for the media giants today.

Text—Can be any form of message, such as verbal, nonverbal communication, visual, and printed information.

Tilt—The ability of the camera lens to move up or down.

Trademark—A distinctive symbol with a unique typeface or graphic element, to create an emblem or logo that distinguishes a company, organization, or institution from another.

Transactional model—A theoretical illustration of a communication theory, characterized by a sender and receiver, and the feedback loop between them.

Transitions—Techniques to move from one shot to another to ensure continuity.

Typography—The selection, arrangement, or use of type.

Vertical integration—The ability of a company to control the production of a media product, from production through distribution to the consumer.

Viewpoint—Describes the distance between the camera and the subject. It includes long shot, medium shot, close-ups, and extreme close-ups.

Visual hierarchy—The prioritizing of visual information, beginning with the focal point.

Watchdog function—The act of supplying information to the public that may serve to inform them of the activities of governments, companies, or individuals usually by citizen or professional journalists

Wipe—A transition that uses a line, or item, which runs across the screen to replace the image previously seen.

World Wide Web—An information system on the Internet, consisting of information packets connected via links.

Web browser—A software application that allows the user to interact with, and use, information on the Web.

Zoom—Altering the focal point of a camera lens, so that the camera appears to get closer to the subject, usually goes from a long shot to a close-up.

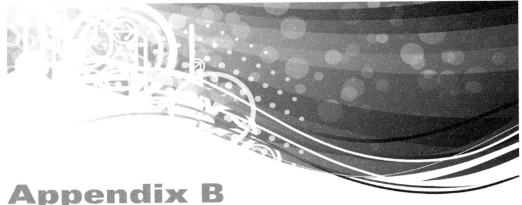

Appendix B
Credits

Chapter graphics

chapter headers #84107278 © Hluboki Dzianis/Shutterstock.com

Chapter 1

children w/ cell phone #141316099 © *Stephen Denness/Shutterstock.com*

Chapter 2

Wall Street Journal Newspaper on Tablet #201326930 ©*Radu Bercan/Shutterstock.com*

World map connection #1718107927 © *Change Hong/Shutterstock.com*

Rupert Murdoch #4234150 © *stocklight/Shutterstock.com*

McDonalds in Russia #1152959990 © *John Williams/Shutterstock.com*

Chinese actress drinking Coca Cola #1720853869 © *supermodel/Shutterstock.com*

Close up of tablet #178166486 © *Eugenio Marongiu/Shutterstock.com*

Students using digital devices #769582051 © *Monkey Business Images/Shutterstock.com*

Man reading paper # 172743683 © *Alexander Raths/Shutterstock.com*

Chapter 3

Figures 1 - 6 © Moses, 2020

Color Wheel Model graphics © Moses, 2000

Chapter 4

Record producer #219751576 © *Dragon Images/Shutterstock.com*

Birds #109467305 © *Mrs. Opossum /Shutterstock.com and* #584892955 © *Gizele/Shutterstock.com*

Signifier/signified © Moses, 2000.

Female with dog # 129639380 © *Ljupco Smokovski /Shutterstock.com*

Stoplight #8096266 © *Vonkara /Shutterstock.com*

Korea reprinted by permission of Dan Reisinger.

Ford ad courtesy Ford Motor Company, global brand licensing

FedEx logo © 2008 FedEx with permission

Tostitos logo provided courtesy of Frito-Lay North America, Inc.

GE logo reprinted with permission of GE.

Chevy logo #306947240 © *Renovacio/Shutterstock.com*

Current BP logo #1212864973 © *Ink Drop/Shutterstock.com*

Old BP logo #1046699740 © *Zenobillis/Shutterstock.com*

KFC logo #620305226 © *AngieYeoh/Shutterstock.com*

KFC logo #1517548217 © *Anakumka/Shutterstock.com*

Man/woman pictographs Symbol Signs American Institute of Graphic Arts (AIGA)

Road signs U.S. Department of Transportation

Department of Transportation pictographs American Institute of Graphic Arts (AIGA)

1976 Olympic symbols © 1976 by Erco Leuchten gmbh

Rio Olympic symbols # 389919376 © *rvlsoft/Shutterstock.com*

Beachfront # 1186745014 © *Musleemin Noitubtim/Shutterstock.com*

Professionals #10584010 © *fd-studio /Shutterstock.com*

Doctors #4133122 © *yanik chauvin/Shutterstock.com*

napkin #517925902 © *NYS/Shutterstock.com*

folded napkins # 1197426427 © *Seregam/Shutterstock.com*

tanks on street #309099071 © *Tamisclao/Shutterstock.com*

Pensive couple #901096 © *Liv Friis-Larson /Shutterstock.com*

Professional group #10166416 © *Gabriel Moisa/Shutterstock.com*

Trojan ad Use of the Trojan® Warrior Head Logo® and EVOLVE.™ trademarks, and EVOLVE print ad for TROJAN® brand Condoms is with the express written permission of Church & Dwight Co., Inc, Princeton, New Jersey. TROJAN, EVOLVE, and the Warrior Head logo are trademarks of Church & Dwight Virginia Co., Inc. © Church & Dwight Virginia Co., Inc. 2007

Chapter 5

Audience #1111341338 © *Anton Gvozdikov/Shutterstock.com*

Dodge Caravan ad   Courtesy Chrysler LLC.

Layout graphics © Moses, 2000.

Line drawing of car # 1246688416 © *yuRomanovich/Shutterstock.com*

Poster drink. Drive. Spill. © Craig Frazier. Reprinted with permission.

Poster from Musical Arts Center courtesy Musical Arts Center

Negative Space one milliom # 1236810967 © *artyway/Shutterstock.com*

Weightlifter #1521875393 © *Improvisor/Shutterstock.com*

Dog show poster © Moses, 2008.

Color wheel #242513875 © *aekikuis/Shutterstock.com*

Child abuse poster © Denver Department of Health & Hospitals. Reprinted with permission.

Layout graphics, © Moses, 2008.

Futura 1930   © 2008 Morla Design, Inc.

Education icons #1160190376 © *Palsur/ Shutterstock.com*

Floral photo #2424097 © Aceshot / *Shutterstock.com.*

Floral graphic #12547207© © *Telnora Olya/ Shutterstock.com*

Elegant woman w/ pearls # 326637986 © *Syda Productions/ Shutterstock.com*

Nostalgic food signs # 202056913 © *lukeruk/ Shutterstock.com*

Lighthouse photo #13017085 © Larry Westberg/*Shutterstock.com*

Lighthouse drawing #4974253 © Michael Vigliotti/*Shutterstock.com*

Lighthouse sketch #3452793 © Markus Gann/*Shutterstock.com*

Lighthouse rough #3307819   © Scott A. Frangos/*Shutterstock.com*

Lighthouse primitive #403752 © Kathleen Good//*Shutterstock.com*

Lighthouse icon #5378035 © aranzazu cueva santa nacher mullet//*Shutterstock.com*

Cat woman # 2303287 © *Andrey Armyagov/Shutterstock.com*

Bonfire # 211091626 © *Fotovika/Shutterstock.com*

Trojan ad Use of the Trojan® Warrior Head Logo® and EVOLVE.™ trademarks, and EVOLVE print ad for TROJAN® brand Condoms is with the express written permission of Church & Dwight Co., Inc, Princeton, New Jersey. TROJAN, EVOLVE, and the Warrior Head logo are trademarks of Church & Dwight Virginia Co., Inc. © Church & Dwight Virginia Co., Inc. 2007

Chapter 6

Mother and baby #12347833 © Svetlana Mihailova/ *Shutterstock.com*

Laughing horse #3338540 © Ovidiu Iordachi/ *Shutterstock.com*

Bridge and sailboat from Photo CD Gallery 2

Abbey # 1122877667 © *MNStudio/Shutterstock.com*

Girl on beach #228941 © *Angie Chauvin/Shutterstock.com*

Harsh flash from Photo CD Gallery 2

Better lighting from Photo CD Gallery 2

Lipsticks # 69743560 © *Africa Studio/Shutterstock.com*

Harsh daylight from Photo CD Gallery 2

Eiffel tower day and night from Key Photos

Cowgirl from Key Photos

Buffalo harbor series, © Moses, 2000.

Cat woman #303287 © *Andrey Armyagov/Shutterstock.com*

Chapter 7

Man reading newspaper #8595004 © *Kateryna Larina/Shutterstock.com*

Woman using phone on subway #1038574906 © *Rawpixel.com/Shutterstock.com*

Couple watching scary movie #77281492 © *Sergey Peterman/Shutterstock.com*

Media globe #12553684 © *Saniphoto/Shutterstock.com*

Internet Network #1563192715 © *Blue Planet Studio/Shutterstock.com*

Old film reels #159328565 © *Serg64/Shutterstock.com*

Elderly man reading newspaper # 600382001 © *sebra/Shutterstock.com*

Bodybuilder man & woman # 102013306 © *Valeriy Lebedev/Shutterstock.com*

Body issues #295695479 © *Studio Menno/Shutterstock.com*

Positive body image #1277154823 © *Jacob Lund/Shutterstock.com*

Wall Street journal newspaper #639656020 © *Hadrian/Shutterstock.com*

USA Today # 1668092182 © *pio3/Shutterstock.com*

Rochester Democrat and Chronicle, October 10, 2020. Copyright © 2020 Gannett-Community Publishing. All rights reserved. Used under license.

Woman looking at magazine #87998674 © *wavebreakmedia/Shutterstock.com*

Life magazines #578069955 © *Ralf Liebhold/Shutterstock.com*

Vintage microphone # 140398567 © *rangizzz/Shutterstock.com*

Old radio #1174405 © *Karla Caspari/Shutterstock.com*

Studio microphone #1571049742 © *Anton27/Shutterstock.com*

Movie clapper #531022507 © *korkut kazcin/Shutterstock.com*

Film camera #4292842 © *Troy Lochner/Shutterstock.com*

Storyboard #1445628302 © *smolaw/ Shutterstock.com*

Mount Rushmore 1 from Key Photos

Mount Rushmore 2 from Key Photos

Mount Rushmore 3 from Key Photos

Buckingham palace, front #13399933 © *justobjects/Shutterstock. com*

Buckingham palace, side #1388195 © *Stephen Finn/Shutterstock.com*

Park bench series #1693681 © *Andreas Guskos/Shutterstock.com*

Couple talking #8431834 © *Sandra G/Shutterstock.com*

Cuts from couple image #8431834© *Sandra G/Shutterstock.com*

Couple on beach #12614398 © *Yuri Arcurs/Shutterstock.com*

Old house from Key Photos

New house #2662688 © *Jeff Thrower (Web Thrower)/Shutterstock.com*

Wipe example #162576146 © *wavebreakmedia/Shutterstock.com*

Camera tilt graphic #13152598 © *Willee Cole/Shutterstock.com*

Camera on crane # 46030954 © *AMA/Shutterstock.com*

TV #357968483 © *Ruslan Ivantsov/ Shutterstock.com*

Boy watching television # 357040109 © *KaliAntye/ Shutterstock.com*

Smart city #1489015757 © *metamorworks/Shutterstock.com*

Man on computer #291976769 © *ruigsantos/Shutterstock.com*

Man wearing headphones #1627288807 © *Ranta Images/Shutterstock.com*

Chapter 8

Woman brain processing #1024742593 © *pathdoc/Shutterstock.com*

Light bulb idea #184763024 © *EFKS/Shutterstock.com*

Puzzled brain # 185695028 © *gabydesign/Shutterstock.com*

Duncan Hines ad Registered mark of Pinacle Food Group LLC, used with permission.

Bedroom interior #1048956431 © *Gaf_Lila/Shutterstock.com*

Henredon Courtesy Natchez Collection from Henredon

SUV © # 678073594 *REDPIXEL.PL/Shutterstock.com*

Landscape painting # 2589656 © *Gino Santa Maria/Shutterstock.com*

Gestalt black and white illustration #1714193686 © *Amiit/Shutterstock.com*

Icons Set 1 #168761525 © *Smart Design/Shutterstock.com*

Icons Set 2 #168761525 © *Smart Design/Shutterstock.com*

Highway logo #331906349 © *musicalryo/Shutterstock.com*

Books in star System to Access Resources (S.T.A.R.) logo for the Dallas Public Library. Design: Brett Baridon. By Permission

Wanderlust logo # 1026433243 © Sloth Astronaut/*Shutterstock.com*

Bubble gum #1130014 © *Todd Taulman/Shutterstock.com*

Ferratella's Lawn Grooming Design Firm: Harp and Company; Client: Joseph Ferratella; Designers: Douglas G. Harp, Linda E. Wagner and Scott McFarland.

Chapter 9

Three gear icon #417078544 © *Piter Kidanchuk/Shutterstock.com*

Woman with shopping bags #1385003768 © *Odua Images/Shutterstock.com*

Emotional facial expressions #1061641181 © *Eshma/Shutterstock.com*

Food donation box # 138508163 © *photka/Shutterstock.com*

Group of men # 1703026933 © *ASDF_MEDIA/Shutterstock.com*

Heart hands #82209640 © Peshkova/*Shutterstock.com*

Boy slapping face #4150423 © Kateryna Potrokhova/*Shutterstock.com*

Credits

Appendix C

Index